CW00449539

Tales from Harbour
The Oral and Folk Story Tradition
Of
Western Notre Dame Bay,
north east coast of Newfoundland Island

Collected, researched and retold

By
Ronald Lloyd Ryan, DA., PhD

VOLUME 1

Contents

Tales from Harbour Divine
The Oral and Folk Story Tradition Of Western Notre Dame Bay,
north east coast of Newfoundland Island

3

4

Tales from Harbour Divine
*The Oral and Folk Story Tradition Of Western Notre Dame Bay,
north east coast of Newfoundland Island*

The Context

The stories in this collection are genuine stories from the people and of the people in the villages of the western extremity of Notre Dame Bay, there on the north east coast, the Beothuck Coast, of Newfoundland Island.

Many of the stories were collected when I was a child, when I didn't know that I was collecting stories of my people. But I absorbed the stories, maybe because I heard them so many times.

Others of the stories I had heard only once or twice - or only half-heard because I wasn't meant to hear - and required considerable research with living persons and with printed historical and cultural sources in order to piece the full story together.

Some of the people who provided me with stories and related information have been acknowledged on the next page.

These stories are not necessarily in their permanent and final form. As with the original folk sources, the stories will change as new information becomes available.

Disclaimer

Although the stories in this series are authentic folk stories from Western Notre Dame Bay, sometimes it has been necessary to change the names, dates, and locations of some of the people and events in order not to invade privacy. Thus, from that perspective, these stories should now be considered works of fiction. Every effort has been made to fictionalize and disguise the original characters even though, in most cases, the oral tradition retained real names. Any resemblances to real people, living or dead, are now inadvertent and coincidental. The only exception is that I have freely used the names of my own ancestors.

Storytellers Roll Of Honour

Roberts Arm, the village which nurtured me, such as it was, was fortunate to have a large group of outstanding and exceptionally skilled story-tellers. It is with enormous gratitude and pride that I will now list some of the best-known of them. Although they are now passed on across the great divide to the mysteries of eternity, I remember them fondly, and with gratitude and affection:

Abner Anthony (Unkl'Ab)

William Anthony (Unkl'Bill)

John Anthony (Unkl'John)

Thirza Anthony (Aunt Turzer)

Thomas Castle (Ole Tom)

Roy Coish (Coishie)

Hurbert Hibbs (Unkl'Bert)

Henry (Harry) Heath (Unkl 'Arry)

Robert LeDrew (Bobler'drew)

William Lush (Skipper Bill)

William Oxford (Unkl' Billy)

Elieu Parsons (Liar Parsons)

Marmion Paddock (Marm)

Samuel Paddock (Skipper Sam)

Lloyd Paddock (Skipper Lloyd)

Agustus Rowsell (Gussy)

Samuel Rowsell (Woody-leg Sam)

James Rideout (Unkl'Bunn)

Edmund Ryan (Unkl'Ed, Gang)

Ronald Ryan (Teakettle)

Stella Gladys Ryan (Stella Maid)

Bernard Ryan (Bern)

Hughie Ryan, Sr. (Larr)

James Ryan (Jimmy)

James Tizzard

Samuel Short

Eric Watkins

Obediah Winsor (Ooby)

The Outport Oral Tradition: Storytelling

Note: Harbour Divine, the fictional village of the following discourse and of most of the stories in this folk story series is meant to be neither a cover for a particular community nor necessarily a composite of any specific collection of the villages of western Notre Dame Bay. It is definitely a movable feast, something like Professor Ted Russel's *Pigeon Inlet* of Uncle Mose fame. It is, at the same time, although not a particular village but all of them put together. Although the village of Harbour Divine has a specific geographical location for purposes of the stories, it could easily be located almost anywhere from Leading Tickles or Fortune Harbour to the south, to Cape John to the north. The people of this area have substantially common ancestry (Beothuck), customs, traditions, language, values, occupations, religion, and world view.

My natal home was a small seaside village, Roberts Arm, isolated and lost in the Newfoundland coastal, mountain and forest wilderness, away from the mainstream of virtually everything that today's literary royalty might consider cultural. Long before the days of radio and TV, let alone highways and motor vehicles, the people of that village, like those of the surrounding communities, had to devise their own entertainments and manners of being.

The Oral and Folk Story Tradition Of Western Notre Dame Bay,
north east coast of Newfoundland Island

Our outport Christmas celebrations may now be well known, at least by cliché, by some folklorists, literati, and media personalities, although never experienced. Those who lived there, though, in those tiny villages, and those who remain fondly remember the cherished traditions: the house-to-house carol singing at Christmas Eve, Christmas night, New year's Eve, New Year's night, and Old Christmas Eve; the mummers throughout the twelve nights of the Yule season; and the school and community concerts - and the occasional *time*, either around Christmas or at other points of the year. But, these were public events, more or less, and have been described elsewhere, more or less, mostly in cliché form, regrettably, wherein the putative participants are somehow presented as simpletons, not as the vibrant, creative, lively and intelligent people that they really were.

Unfortunately, much that has been, and is still being, proffered as outport culture is cliché and trite, written by people who never experienced the reality, however humble. Much that is presented as outport culture I don't recognize, it being both overly simplistic and uni-dimensional, and does not even begin to capture the complexity of outport social organization and culture that was influential in my own development, for example. Naturally, I have no way of knowing whether the culture and mores of my childhood and youth were unique, or whether too few people are writing about the real culture of their own natal outports, or both.

In any case, what is presented as Newfoundland culture disturbs me because, firstly, in many instances, there seems to be a condescending attitude towards these *poor, ignorant, quaint, lazy, simple people.*

It fact, it was not like that! These people were highly intelligent, hard working - almost non-stop working, in fact, both males and females – proud, independent, and, at least some of them, fun-loving and creative. Although it may be true that these people were unlettered and monetarily poor, they were not poor in spirit. Above all, they were recyclers of the first order. Almost no resources were wasted. Moreover, they were outstandingly innovative when they experienced everyday problems of trying to exist, to make a living. Not all of these characteristics, of course, were to their economic benefit.

In particular, what seems to be lesser known, in Newfoundland and Labrador provincial literary circles, is the more intimate family circle venue of the oral tradition, in particular, the *storytelling* tradition and practices of the people of western Notre Dame Bay or, simply, Green Bay. Before the advent of Radio and, later, television, and before the coming of the roads, storytelling was the mainstay of diversion in almost every household, with the family gathered around the open fireplace, in the earliest days, or, in later days, around the *Waterloo* or *Comfort* or *New Ensign* stove after the family managed to gather sufficient resources to purchase such a modern contrivance, or managed to convince the merchant that if they bought it, *on tik,* they would be able to pay it of – eventually. Some maybe luckless went to their graves with their stove still not paid for.

Even when radio transmissions became available, few people had radios, and even those who did turned them on at 8:30 in the morning for the news and Morning devotions. Then they turned them off again. The radio was used again for another half hour from 6:30 to 7:00 in the evening, again for news. The battery that was purchased after the fishermen arrived home from the Labrador in October ($11.00 - $13.00 at Nhimsheiaha Hewlett's General Store) had to last until the following Autumn.

Sometimes, if the battery were prematurely exhausted, it was possible with some of them to perk them up a little. If the battery were placed on the stove top and allowed to slowly warm up until quite hot and if they didn't explode before the magic could be effected, it was sometimes possible to wiggle out the carbon core. In the hole, one could pour Minard's Liniment, a patent medicine of the time, and the carbon core pushed back in. It was possible to get another month or so of service from the battery by such a remedy. The completely exhausted battery would be tossed out into the landwash where some opportunistic children might extract and chew the pitch, thinking that it was just another form of *BlackJack Gum*, a licorice flavoured chewing gum that was popular at the time. Why those children never died from poisoning, I'll never figure out. *I'm* still here!

Sometimes, the only light was from the stove, or from crudely made sheep tallow candles or from a small oil lamp on the kitchen table - in the early days fueled with rancid seal oil or rendered out blubber, equally rancid - wafting its cloying aroma throughout the house. Not that anybody noticed anything unusual. In these now far-off days, seal blubber soap, made in the kitchen by the lady of the house, was the only soap available for laundry or for personal hygiene. Everybody reeked of seal blubber because it permeated their clothing, their bedding, their very pores. Moreover, virtually everyone wore seal skin boots and maybe other seal-skin clothing, also adding their sour pissey smell to the accumulated cooked fish and roasted Beaver and other strong smells of the humble dwellings, socks and mitts hanging over the stoves adding their distinctive flavours to the overall and ubiquitous aromas.

Seal blubber had an additional value. In the days when there was no Pablum or infant formula and when mothers could not produce sufficient milk to keep a child alive, a cloth dipped in seal oil was utilized not only as a pacifier for an infant but also as a significant source of nutrition.

But never mind all of these healthy smells. Something much more important was afoot. The elders of the family, the grandparents or visiting relatives, friends, or neighbours, would spin their yarns with the others of the family, including women and children and babes-in-arms, held spellbound in open-mouthed thrall. Sometimes, the content of the storytelling would be detailing of family genealogy: who died when; who remarried; who had a child for her father, or brother; which child was born before the mother was married; or whose father was not the man that the mother had married, and other delightful, informative, and entertaining information.

Always of importance was which girl was in forced servitude (lightly called *out in-service*) and which girl had been *purchased* by which merchant in order to pay off her father's fishing debts, and for how long, and so on, and weather said girl was required to serve as her mistress' birth control method. Concubinage was practiced until quite late in history, although it was hardly ever talked about. Also detailed was how many wives some particular

*The Oral and Folk Story Tradition Of Western Notre Dame Bay,
north east coast of Newfoundland Island*

man had had and how many husbands individual women had buried, as if there was a husband burying contest of some kind.

That stuff was all important information. One really needed to know one's genealogy, more or less, and it was the recitation of all of the interconnected and sometimes complex and tangled family trees. that helped young people to avoid marrying first cousins if, in fact, it could be avoided. Of course, if it couldn't be helped, then it couldn't be helped. Pragmatism was one of the few articles of dogma with these practical people.

After the family genealogy had once again been recited and hammered out, and quarrels settled, at least for the moment, then *real storytelling* could begin. Stories were abundant and were as varied as were the storytellers. The family and community recognized and acknowledged that some of the storytellers were highly skilled, detailed in their memory, meticulous in detail, and effective and unforgettable in presentation.

It wasn't a requirement that all of the details of a particular story be absolutely true; neither did it have to be original. It turns out, however, that the facts of life at Harbour Divine and of the surrounding villages from which many of the livyers came, had been, and still were, so grim, and so many unusual events had taken place in one village or another, that stories could be true and shiveringly captivating at one and the same time.

The story of Mr. Brookston, living with his family out in that lonely cove, who had delivered his missus's eleven children and had to bury five of them, was old hat, as were the stories of all of the young women who died in childbirth. Of particularly

14

Tales from Harbour Divine
*The Oral and Folk Story Tradition Of Western Notre Dame Bay,
north east coast of Newfoundland Island*

delicious hearing were the deformed babies – the one with a tail, for example, or the one with six toes and six fingers, or the one with two heads, or the one with multiple appendages, or the one with multiple genitalia, all of whom had died instantly, with a palm over the mouth and the nose, and described in the church register, if they were recorded at all, as *still born*, the midwife doing the function entrusted to her by the family and the community.

Occasionally, the conversation would drift to such still-births, of which there seem, from today's perspective, to have been a rather high incidence. Sometimes, doubt would be expressed about whether the number of infant deaths was really necessary, as if there were some choice in the matter. Of course, as everybody knew, there *WAS* some choice in the matter! Although, today, it is an issue that is not discussed, at that time, before doctors and hospitals, and at a time when everybody worked, worked nonstop, it was an issue that had to be considered. The fact was that a child that could not be, ultimately, productive and could not, ultimately, contribute to the family and village, really had no place. So, a defective child died before it cried! That was the mid-wife's function: to make the decision whether a child was viable. If not, it was dispatched immediately by simply smothering, and another still-birth entered the annals of the village .

Because there was, at that time, a high degree of inter-marriage, the infanticide of defectives also served to keep the bloodlines reasonably pure. Whether the pragmatics came from our European or our Aboriginal ancestors, or both, is not important. What is important to note is that it WAS necessary.

Less the reader sniff at the level of intermarriage, it is important to note that the total population of Newfoundland and Labrador trace their European ancestry back to maybe as few as 20,000 people, the original immigrants from Europe, almost all of whom mated with and were absorbed into the Aboriginal population. Moreover, very few immigrants arrived in Newfoundland after about 1830 because Canada and the United States were, by that time, aggressively competing for immigrants, with enormous advertising campaigns in Europe offering free agricultural land, for example. Newfoundland and Labrador could not compete in that department. All that Newfoundland could offer was non-stop, back-breaking, labour.

Because of the intersecting blood lines, one might guess that there may have been some evolutionary regression, a well-known biological phenomenon that is utilized by agronomists to isolate original genetic complexes in order to re-create original blood and genetic lines in cattle and certain seeds, for example. In the remote Newfoundland villages, the process seems to have been occurring naturally. Other sociologists and statisticians call the phenomenon *regression to the mean.*

Several women who were closely related to me, now passed on over Jordan, used to tell me, when I was much younger, about some of their decisions when they acted in the capacity of midwife. One of these women preserved the life of a child by biting off its tail and stitching the wound. It healed along with the umbilicus, and no one was the wiser. Another child was born with three thumbs on each hand. The extra thumbs were likewise bitten off and the wound stitched with sewing yarn. These children grew to adulthood, married and had families. As of this writing, I understand that one is still living. He probably does not know how his life was spared at the first moments of life because the midwife defied convention.

Another lady decided that an extra toe and webbed feet did not constitute deformities. These children who were, consequently, spared are still quite alive, hale, and hearty, now providing emotional succor to their grandchildren and great-grandchildren.

Good storytellers always kept in mind that a good story must, first and foremost, be interesting and entertaining. Crass historical fact should *never* get in the way of a good story! Moreover, these masters of the craft understood that stories are organic. Stories change and grow as the storyteller refines them. Should it turn out that some aspect of a story is not particularly interesting, then that element is summarily dropped. Should the story-teller stumble on an innovation or particularly entertaining embellishment – determined, of course, by the reaction of the listeners - then that aspect stayed.

Good stories always change. Nobody pretends they are gospel. That is why all cultures cherish their storytellers above almost any other single group of people – it was true, then; it is still true today, wherever the culture. Those who insist that stories adhere strictly to cold historical factoids are missing the whole point of storytelling.

Nobody ever suggested that any of the stories lacked veracity or, in fact, contained any. In any case, that was not their concern. The story was the objective, the entertainment. What was appreciated - prized, even - was the skill of the raconteur, not whether the story was absolutely gospel truth or conforming to some narrow historical ideal. About the only imperative aspect of story in these venues was verisimilitude; the stories had to be comprehensible to the people, within the realm of possibilities and practicalities within which these people lived. Even though I heard literally thousands of stories from my ancestors and their compatriots, *tall tales*, as we understand the term today, was almost non-existent as were what we call, today, fairy-tales.

That is not to say that people did not believe in fairies. They did, bringing in to play the notion of fairies and *little people* brought from Europe, as well as the little people that figured highly in the mythology of our Aboriginal ancestors. The denizens of these remote and isolated outport fishing villages also believed in ghosts, tokens and witches – male and female. These phenomenon were accepted as having the same reality as did the source of their religious beliefs. They saw no difference between virgin births, raising people from the dead, and ascending bodily into heaven, on the one hand, and the presence of witches and other supernatural phenomena, on the other. It was all of a piece. People did not classify them differently. If one believed the religious super-naturalism, then it would be contradictory, even hypocrisy, to not believe the supernatural phenomena that they felt all around them.

Almost every village had at least one witch. At Harbour Divine, Carrie Limford was one such and was well-acknowledged. Everybody accepted the fact. Everybody knew that she had

18

Tales from Harbour Divine
The Oral and Folk Story Tradition Of Western Notre Dame Bay,
north east coast of Newfoundland Island

enormous powers which, fortunately, she did not, usually, use to ill ends. If the Witch of Endor had such powers in the Old Testament, why should Carrie Limford have any less? In fact, there was a certain - if muted - pride that Carrie Limford lived in the village. She gave the village a certain status.

Without doubt, Carrie Limford had some detractors. But if some disgruntled people piously quoted the Scriptures about *suffering a witch not to live*, or mentioned how witches were dispatched in Europe and Massachusetts, then Carrie's supporters were quick to counter with the injunction that he who is without sin should throw the first stone. That shut them up and made them pull in their horns!

Now, every person who ever attempted to navigate the environs of Harbour Divine knew about the sunkers at the entrance to the harbour and wisely gave them wide berth, especially at low tide. Sometimes, a careless lad, coming home from sparking a girl at Pilley's Island or Three Arms or Basket Bight or Shark Cove, drunk on love, no doubt, would scrape his keel on the sunkers. In fact, if spring tides and neap tides occurred simultaneously, the kelp of the sunkers would be floating on the surface. But, at high tide, these jagged rocks were five or six feet underwater.

If some careless soul doubted Carrie Limford's powers, a villager wanting to set the doubting Thomas straight would accompany them to visit Carrie Limford when the tide was top high. Hearing the outrageous temerity of the doubter, Carrie would ask him or her to stand at the window and look out the harbour. "Look at where da zunkers be," she would say, "and dem rocks will rise to the surface three times."

The skeptical person would humour the getting-elderly lady by standing at the window, smirk plastered across his insolent face. That smirk soon disappeared, however, when the sunkers breached three times, just like a Grampus! Another unbelieving soul was won to the wonders of witchcraft and the supernatural, and maybe even to Christianity.

In general, the villagers were not overly concerned about Carrie's skills because the remedies were common knowledge. If someone suspected Carrie of using her powers against one, then the remedies could be quickly effected. Carrie knew and respected the knowledge of the villagers. Thus, a rather easy truce existed between Carrie and the other denizens of the tiny Village.

As unusual as it may appear to certain devout religionists, Carrie Limford went to church regularly and even received communion. Several ministers, over the years, had doubted whether it should be permitted, but whether the weak-minded parsons feared their Lord's censure for denying communion to one who exhibited such faith or whether they feared Carrie's powers even more, neither of them dared to deny the suppliant who came to the Lord's table. More pointedly, neither of them, Catholic or Protestant, took the fateful decision to even suggest denying communion or any other pastoral succor to the wise lady.

Not so Chas Barslen, sometimes member of the Board of Session of the Unitarian-flavoured Methodist Church. He took it upon himself to go to Carrie's home and tell her she had no business even going to church let alone desecrating the Lord's Supper. Carrie told Chas to mind his own business and let the

Lord decide whether she was apostate, and that the Bible said that Chas Barslen was not to stand in judgment. He threatened, however, to take the matter up with the Session. Then, he left the house and proceeded to engage in the spring fishery.

Even though the other fishing crews with traps set outside the harbour and at various near berths in the bay were doing well with the fish, Chas Barslen was getting nothing. Absolutely nothing!

"Dass dat bitch auva Carrie Limford," shouted Chas Barslen. "I'll fix her guts!"

So, believing that Carrie was using her powers to prevent him from getting fish, Chas set up the remedy. The remedy against witches is ancient lore and was brought to our shores by our knowledgeable and careful ancestors. Because virtually everyone knows these remedies, it is not necessary to waste the reader's time with detailing them now.

In any case, the days passed. Chas Barslen was still getting no fish. A week passed.

Monday morning, as Chas Barslen was having his breakfast of salted fish and brewis, having just arrived from the fishing grounds with another water haul, a knock sounded on the door. A knock on a door in that village was serious stuff. It always meant trouble of some sort: a politician, mercifully rare; a policeman, even more rare; or the clergyman. A morning knock meant the clergy had bad news or, this morning, Carrie Limford with her hand holding her paining gut.

*The Oral and Folk Story Tradition Of Western Notre Dame Bay,
north east coast of Newfoundland Island*

"Good morning, Carrie!"

"Good morning, Mister Barslen."

"*Mister* Barslen, now, is it?"

"You be throwing away dat stuff, Chas, and you'll be getting feesh. But, no more standin agin me in the Session! Otherwise, I'll 'ole to me ground!"

Chas, recognizing the potential standoff, and fearing a bad fishing season, agreed to Carrie's terms, bid her good morning and returned to the house where his remedy was festering behind the *Waterloo*.

Chas threw his preparation down into the landwash, where the bottle broke against a rock, spewing its stinking contents over the accumulated seashells, soundbones, and other detritus typical of such a location, called his crew together and set off to check his cod traps for the second time that morning. He returned shortly after noon with his skiff riding to the gunnels, midship room and cuddy filled to the brim with cod.

Chas was, until his death, quick to give Carrie credit for the most successful fishing season that he had ever had.

****

These skilled ranconters took their time to develop and relate their stories. It was winter, after all - nobody had time for stories during the summer. Time was long, sometimes, in the winter, especially after dark, sometimes wearying, other times worrying, maybe both contemporaneously, especially if last

22

Tales from Harbour Divine
The Oral and Folk Story Tradition Of Western Notre Dame Bay, north east coast of Newfoundland Island

autumn's potato crop was meager or if the capelin rotted before they could dry properly or if the fish were sunburned or if people realized that they might have to deprive their dogs of the dried squids in order to keep their own souls and bodies connected until the ice broke up and seals struck in.

People didn't want to think about the probabilities of the hungry month of March or any other potentially hungry month. Stories, please! They needed stories. Thus, with time at their disposal, the storytellers could explore the intricacies and complexities and interconnectedness of, and tangents to, their main story, pausing as necessary to listen to questions, responding to queries, straightening out the puzzled, and directing the lost back to the thrust of the revelation.

The queries presented by the listeners were *never - never ever!* -designed to expose the story-teller to ridicule or to suggest that the latter was attempting to deceive. Questions were authentic efforts to ensure that the storyteller was being consistent, although that word was not in their vocabulary. Consistency in the story was a point of religion with these people, particularly among the non-churchgoers. While the church-goers had a certain reliance and consistency based on their articles of faith, these generally non-church-goers, or those who were in, at most, casual attendance, relied on their own source of consistency. Consistency in the storyteller's narrative meant that the world of these people was still orderly and, thus, reliable, not capricious. They had more inconsistencies and caprice and insecurity than they could comfortably deal with in their daily affairs. Stories was the major artifice utilized to bring together the disparate uncontrollable factors of life and make them to, at least, *seem* manageable, to *appear* orderly, to have the aura of rationality, and to persuade them that God was not capricious, after all..

When, in explanatory response to their concerns, the story teller eased away their fear or puzzlement, the gentlemen present, as well as many of the women, would shake their heads in relief, nod in agreement, and suck or smack their lips in appreciation, much as if they had just eaten a fresh strawberry - thus reminding all present, if anyone cared to notice, that they still carried strongly many of the mannerisms of their not-so-distant Aboriginal ancestors - Beothuck, Nascopi, and even Micmac, and Inuit. They might, also, say, "Aw!" clearly expressing their relief that the story still hung together, consistency was still apparent, and that all was still right with the world.

The *listeners* had much invested in their ensuring that they said or did nothing to suggest that there was anything out of balance with the story then being related. Firstly, they were anxious that the storyteller not lose face or be offended. If that happened, the storyteller might simply stop and not relate the story further.

Moreover, as sometimes happened if the raconteur were thusly rudely interrupted, he might say something like "certainly, Jaesus, you know the story better than I do, so you can fuckin' well tell it" - which did not constitute swearing because they had been provoked. In such a circumstance, the interrupter would lose face, be embarrassed, and have to back down, maybe be even obliged to leave the gathering. Of course, another reason for wanting the story to continue unabated was that the listeners wanted to hear all of the story. Moreover, if one heard the story in sufficient detail, then in a future circumstance, he - sometimes she - could be the centre of attention and gain face by having an air-tight story to impart. Above all, if it were a good story, if it hung together, if it maintained interest, if it in someway presented the cultural group in some new, and maybe even positive light - although that latter criterion was not a necessary one, then the listener would be more secure of his individual and his group place in the grand scheme of things. Storytelling was the core of their cultural identity and of their true religion.

In general, the story-tellers were not church goers; the storytellers were shunned by those who did. The stpry-tellers believed in fun; they were not dour like their Christian brethren who believed that if something was the least bit funny then it had to be sinful.

They were nominally Christian, but animist in practice

They were nominally Protestant, although many of them were Roman Catholic by disposition and, to tell the absolute truth, by ancestry, albeit partially - on the European side of their genesis, anyhow. Their Irish Catholic Huguenot background is a story unto itself.

Some of these men who considered themselves Catholic - although never having graced the inside of a Catholic church, were in fact, Orangemen. Being Orangemen gave them something to do on Saturday nights, and it was an outlet for their creative pursuits related to composing songs and plays. Imagine the double take of the Grandmaster of the Orange association when the certificates of these men with Irish Catholic names crossed his desk for official signature affixing.

They went to church rarely except for funerals, preferably only their own; rarely for weddings, not wanting to be witness to the downfall of the son of some other man, unless the son happened to be their own, in which case, the son was demonstrating his maturity and, undoubtedly, had chosen well, had chosen, no doubt, a paragon of virtue like his own mother, or unless the bride happened to be their own daughter, in which case, lucky the man who had managed to capture her affections. With any luck, the woman would soon whip him in shape and make a man of him.

These unlettered, untutored men recognized that the scriptural stories did not hang together – at least not in their opinions - did not create a seamless whole, contained much too much inconsistency. They compensated with their own seamless web of story telling, incorporating their paradigm of the physical world as well as the spiritual – the latter full of ghosts, tokens, fairies, angels, devils, spirits in the wind, and maybe, just maybe, a god of some description somewhere. They rejected notions of Hell but gave lip-service to the possibility of a heaven. The latter made for good stories, anyhow.

These men pitied those who did believe the religious and doctrinal details, rather than practice the generalities as the storytellers did, and perceived the religious latter as weaklings, especially the clergy. Those paragons of dubious virtue they pitied most of all, but the storytellers were always willing to entertain him - or possibly her, in the case of the Salvation Army.

26

Tales from Harbour Divine
*The Oral and Folk Story Tradition Of Western Notre Dame Bay,
north east coast of Newfoundland Island*

These people, after all were the most deluded, the stunnest of the works. Fortunately, they didn't have to entertain any of the clergy very often because the clergy came to visit during the day when the storytellers were working. Rare the clergyman who would dare to visit a netloft or stage head. Might get "stuff" on their holy hands, you know!

These storytellers also, moreover, probably acknowledged to themselves that when they lay dying in their own beds - if they got that chance, most of them expecting to die somehow while they still had their boots on - they would allow their respective dim-witted clergyperson to lead them to the throne of grace that they didn't believe in; receive assurance of their redemption, which they did not perceive themselves as needing because they had little or no concept of sin as long as they did not do anything deliberately to hurt somebody else; and even go so far as to receive a drop of grape juice for a last communion when what they really would have preferred was a good snort of black run.

Some of the number of this unique band of men and women would, sooner or later, get religious, or their spouse would succumb to the persuasion of religion. Then these erstwhile storytellers would typically abandon their colleagues because the latter (a) smoked, (b) they swore, (c) they drinked, (d) they used blagard, (d) they were ignarnt, (e) they were unbelievers, and the good Lord had told them, as it said in their Bibles, to *get ye out from among them.*

So, the former sinners, now with pursed-lipped indignation and sour countenances, went to church to praise their God who didn't enjoy or appreciate story-telling, while their sinner friends were telling their stories, and laughing and carrying on and enjoying life because, as they would be quick to remind anyone who was interested, *their* Bible told them that Jesus said, "I have come that you might have life more abundantly" and turned water into wine that made people drunk, and that Jesus told stories to help the abundant life along, just as they were now doing.

Harbour Divine, at one time, had as many ghosts as people, and they were regularly experienced in houses and in other places where the ancestors and ancients had congregated. Likewise, fairies were hiding behind almost tree. Sometimes, men and children became lost in the wilderness – led astray by fairies seeking favours – and were returned to their homes only when the lost souls turned their pockets inside out to demonstrate to the fairies that they were as poor as the fairies themselves or, otherwise, when they shared their lunch with these diminutive and unseen denizens of the forests.

Wise people, before going into the woods, always took a crust of bread and placed it in some discrete location so that the fairies could find it. These people never became lost - not for very long anyway - and always checked, when they were wending their way home, to see if the fairies had taken their offerings. Invariably, the offerings had been accepted, and the fairies had held to their promise not to lead astray anyone who provided such respectful morsels.

Fairies also seem to have had another attribute that was whispered about, and that was impregnating older girls and young women, but always talked about when the younger children were snug in their feather beds, although the scruping of the bed-ropes might suggest that they were not asleep but were straining to catch every last word of what was being said in the kitchen.. It seems that maidens who went into the woods by themselves soon found themselves "in the family way," and the children of the family learned that Sally, or Molly, or Jemima was going to have a baby, begotten on her by the fairies, and let that be a lesson to other young girls not to go into the woods by themselves. Strangely, the babies of fairy fathers always seemed as fully human as the other people of the village. Strange, too, was the fact that most of these fairy begattings seemed to occur after the young men returned from their Labrador fisheries, although there never seemed to be any real acknowledged connection between the two phenomena. Funny about that!

****

It was also amazing to note the sexual prowess of Newfoundland men, especially when compared with the clearly effeminate so-called men from places such as England and the United States. Why, a man from Newfoundland could (ahem ... impregnate, although that is not the word that would have been used !!!) numerous nubile maidens in a single night (!!!). When their counterparts from those other, rich, countries would be absolutely exhausted !!!! the Newfoundlander was still "rarin and ready to go," main boom still at the ready.

****

A tremendous tradition of story-telling grew up in the various churches, particularly in the testimony meetings of the Pentecostals and the Salvation Army as well as in the Unitarian-Methodist (later, United Church) after-services. Many of the faithful who stood to witness to the saving power of their Lord and Saviour also took advantage of the opportunity to publicly confess various and sundry sins both of commission and thought. Curiously, very few ever confessed to sins of omission. Nevertheless, the stories that were related in religious services ranged all the way from implicit adultery to theft to arson and to behaviours which ranged from the deplorable to the ludicrous. Many times, people would express the opinion that confession might be good for the soul, but it had no business being expressed publicly. Life still went on and stories still continued to be related in the various churches.

An acquaintance remembers when one of the Methodist faithful declared himself an apostate because on a particular Sunday morning he didn't go to church because the coastal vessel was due to arrive and he wanted to see who was on it; that he had, in effect, taken the coastal vessel for his god, at least on that occasion. Another faithful comrade related how he had taken the last 25 cents in the house and bought himself a plug of *Beaver* tobacco when his children were crying for food. Another claimed that he was so *happy in the Lord* that he could go "hand over hand over the beams" [of the church] and that he could "go through Hell's flames with a brin bag of dryed grass on his back and not scarch a bleade." For a people who insisted that the Bible be read literally and who wouldn't recognize a simile or metaphor if one were to clout them in the head with a 2 X 4, they were masters of imagery and linguistic subtlety.

Regardless of one's feelings over the appropriateness of the stories - in testimonies and prayers - one thing is certain:

these unlettered people learned the art of story telling to a very high degree, using metaphor and imagery so skillfully that the respective congregations were held spell-bound by their comrades' revelations!

Of particular interest were the dreams and visions that the various members of the congregation would relate to the faithfully assembled. Some of these visions were so unquestioningly accepted that the community could be in turmoil for months!

The other major venue for storytelling were the stage lofts and boat-building sheds, especially during the long snowy months when little could be done out of doors. As men repaired their skiffs or mended or knitted new nets, stories would be going on non-stop. Some of these stories, while implicitly sexual in some way, maybe, frequently had overtones of rudimentary ethical questioning. Given that these men generally had little or no formal education – well, actually, no education at all that the world would recognize as such - and that few of them could read, even if they might be able to *draw or sketch their neams* - their ability to engage in philosophical discourse might be surprising keeping in mind, of course, that these things are relative. As commonly realized in academic circles – claimed, anyway - there seems to be a very strict limit to the ability of unlettered people to engage in such discourse, sophisticated thought being a function of language development, linguistic facility and expertise in the rules of predicate logic.

Take, for example, the story about Uncle Soddy Middleton, who had out-lived all four wives and all of his children and was relying on the tender ministrations of his nephew's daughter – *so homely that one look from her could cause tar to scale off the side of a punt.* Apparently, the young woman became "in the family way" for the elderly gentleman, so the story went, anyway, or, at least, we were supposed to believe.

Invariably, one of the men, while mending his nets, would make some comment such as, "Boy, he mustiabeen well up, den!" and the silence would hang as everybody absorbed the full significance of the double meanings.

Another man would rejoin, "As, sur, he could hardly get his hand up, let alone . . . . Garge you got a light fer me pipe?" and there would be a general guffaw at the new *double entendre.*

The story would continue with the observation that the child born of the doubtful union looked suspiciously like the young man that the maiden married after uncle Soddy died, shortly after his supposed sexual exploit - exhausted him, one might say. Another man would add, "Yes, but, now, the child looked like Uncle Soddy when *he* was a young man and her husband is a relative of Uncle Soddy, anyhow."

The story would usually end on the note that even if Uncle Soddy did manage to get his hand on the girl's ..... ahem, cheek! ... then the old man's imagination could have done the rest, sufficiently so that when he finally expired, he left his house and all of his worldly goods and wealth to his young housekeeper.

In fact, one man would say knowingly, "Well, you know, he left her a small fartchin - over 63 dollars. When she paid five dollars for a pine box and five dollars for the parson and three dollars for the gravediggers, she still had fifty dollars left. That is as much - or more - than a shareman can expect to clear after a full season's fishing on the Labrador. If Uncle Soddy did managed to touch her ... ahem, cheek!" . . . at which point he would take the lifter, remove the top cover of the stove, spit in his baccy juice, turn around and grin .... "Then, what harm was done?"

Someone would go on to say, "Well, she's now a happily married woman and the mother of several beautiful children. Why that girl of 'earn is almost as beautiful as the mother!" to the general outburst of laughter all around.

Family Myths

Another delicious aspect of storytelling was the transmission of cherished family myths, Every family had some story that defined their lineage and gave them dignity. Either they were descendant from royalty - some royal family from some country. It didn't really matter just which. Or, they were the offspring of stowaways, or of pirates. It didn't really matter who. A pirate is somebody, after all, and had to work for a living just as a royal person had to. Indeed, the pirate had to work much harder! Being the offspring of a pirate was not to be sneezed at; it was to be a source of pride.

Or large sums of money were lying and going fousty in the Bank of England, just waiting to be claimed by the family. Or they could claim that some family member had performed some prodigious feat of strength, or intelligence or wit or sexual prowess; or they knew about hidden treasure, presumably belonging to pirate great grandfathers. The great pirate Peter Easton did live in Newfoundland, after all, and it is (or at least, used to be) amazing the number of families that could trace their direct ancestry - although through the women, to be sure - back to that esteemed cut-throat.

Of particularly importance was how love was so strong that a girl became *in the family way* even though she had never lain with her lover, the fact that her bedroom was on the ground floor and her room easily entered through a window, notwithstanding.

Another family myth would explain how the dark skin and dark hair of the family was due not at all to any trace of Indian blood - "my goodness, no, we are not related to savages" - but, in actual fact, was due to an old grandmother who was Spanish or Portuguese. The embarrassment of Aboriginal ancestry was such that it had to be covered up some way, *when in actual fact* virtually every family had as much more Aboriginal – what used to be called Native - blood as they had European, the latter being of such a remove that the only residual being the European name. But, these people did have European names, names that could be traced back to English or Irish villages, and these names were precious, and the more honour that could be attributed to these names, the more honour accrued to the family, never mind the dirt and the poverty and the malnutrition currently extant.

Myths are *always* stories with some basis in actual fact, but were sufficiently fictionalized to make them interesting and to bring honour to the family, although the details of the stories might not stand up to close historical scrutiny. But history is little more than embellished myth, and is always designed to bring honour to the nation of the author and to the author himself (or herself). So we have nothing to be ashamed of in that regard. In fact, we should be proud of our family myths; we should cherish them, and we should continue relating them every chance we get, and change them as necessary to make them even more interesting.

As educated people have known for generations, people's identities reside in their myths. Several well-known psychologists have recently called for the creation of more and greater and more-empowering myths. The stronger the myths, the stronger the family, the stronger the society, the stronger the culture, the more empowered the individual.

****

Issues

Some people say that storytelling is a lost art. I'm not at all sure that that is anywhere near true. People still tell stories. The subject matter may be different: "Did you like the dress that Brittany was wearing at the party when William scorned her on the last episode of *The Wrong and the Faithless?* for example. In fact, I will argue that storytelling is more important, now, than it ever has been before, primarily because people are now more socially disconnected than ever before, despite the Internet and social media, and storytelling may be the single most significant sustained means by which human social connectedness is maintained. Historically and traditionally it may have come naturally because people spent most of their time together in

Tales from Harbour Divine
*The Oral and Folk Story Tradition Of Western Notre Dame Bay,
north east coast of Newfoundland Island*

35

relatively small social groups; now, it may be that it has to be contrived (movies, plays, soaps, raves, church, etc.) all of which have elements of story.

The listener?

It may not be a matter of story *telling* being the lost art, but of story *listening*. Story telling may be declining because there are few listeners. Listening to story is an art form in itself. The major difference between television story telling, for example, and the oral tradition form of storytelling is that the listener in front of the TV set can be passive. On doesn't have to think, simply absorb. In contrast, when one is listening to a story, via the oral tradition, the listener has to share in the construction of the story with the storyteller. The story teller will, typically, set the scene very briefly. He or she is counting on the listener to then construct the story context for oneself. Moreover, the story teller may depend on the listeners to ask appropriate questions not only to assist the listener in understanding the crucial elements of the story, but to assist the storyteller, the necessary feedback loop assuring the story-teller that he or she is conveying the story as intended.

Questioning

The art of listening includes the art of questioning. But, the questions have to be helpful to the story. "Is the story true?" is not a helpful question. All stories are true in the same manner that a piece of visual art is true. In the same manner that a piece of visual art has to be selective in what is conveyed, so too has a story have to be selective. Neither can ever be comprehensive.

"Who was that, really?" or "Did this really happen?" are also not helpful questions in listening to a story any more than one would ask that of a TV show. The TV will not answer the question. The story-teller will reveal the necessary information as he or she deems appropriate. It is disruptive to ask such questions of the story-teller.

"I notice that you didn't tell the story the same way before." exhibits a misunderstanding of where the story resides between tellings. The storyteller *knows* the story but he or she has not memorized the story. Thus, each time a story is related, it has to be reconstructed. The essentials of the story will be retained, the details may change. Besides, as noted above, it is the story-teller's prerogative to change the story as deemed necessary to make the story more interesting.

Lies, history, or gossip?

These three: lies, history, and gossip, are probably the most dangerous demons of storytelling. The simplest one is the issue of lies. The person who sees stories as lies has missed the point of story completely. In fact, a fictional story may convey more absolute truth that a so-perceived non-fictional "story" could ever achieve. Stories are not documentaries, and make no related pretense. The first rule of storytelling is entertainment. All other issues, such as moralizing or presenting cultural knowledge place a distant second. If it doesn't entertain, if people do not enjoy the story, then go do something useful and leave storytelling to people who can tell stories and do not apologize for it.

History? I told a story in a group setting. I though I fulfilled my purpose. The listeners seemed to enjoy the experience and some were even animately involved, helping me construct the story. Afterwards, however, one of the gathering approached me, explained that he was an amateur historian and wanted me to provide certain specific details because he wanted to go to some or other archives and get "complete" information. He was crestfallen and upset when I explained that I made no attempt to convey detailed history, that I had deliberately fictionalized certain personalities and events in order to protect privacy. Clearly, he didn't understand story.

There is another related problem: History? There is no such thing. There are only histories (note the plural!). There are as many histories as there are people purporting to be historians, amateur or otherwise. History is not a hard science. Maybe it should be, but it is not. Facts do not constitute history. History is a matter of selecting certain facts considered relevant and interpreting them in a very idiosyncratic manner. Every historian will look at the same set of facts and interpret them differently. Story is above history. Story is below history. Story gets at the crux of history while leaving the details to be interpreted by others.

Gossip?

Is story gossip?

Yes! And no!

38

Tales from Harbour Divine
*The Oral and Folk Story Tradition Of Western Notre Dame Bay,
north east coast of Newfoundland Island*

Most effective storytellers will deliberately fictionalize for a host of reasons, not the least of which is to protect privacy and to protect sources. Moreover, by fictionalizing personalities and events, the storyteller has a much larger slate on which to draw his or her picture, unhampered by an untimely death or an uncooperative subject. Many people, upon hearing a story, will ask, "Who was that?" In other words, that person wants to reduce story to gossip. Such a listener assumes that the story is about one or more people who could be named. In actuality, the story is almost always about everyone, about general propensities and proclivities of people in general that the storyteller will embody in selected fictional subjects.

Besides, the storyteller doesn't want to get sued. He has an obligation to protect the real people who by their behaviour have managed to portray the general human condition that we all share. The successful storyteller will enable his listeners to see themselves, while painting a fictional picture of an "other."

Storytelling and story writing

There are enormous differences between storytelling orally, having interactive listeners, and portraying the same story in written form. This issue could be addressed in such a comprehensive manner that a 500 page book could result. Here, it will suffice only to say that maybe the most important differences are (a) more care has to be taken in setting the context because the story writer cannot assume that the readers will share a sufficient common background which would enable appreciation and enjoyment of the story, and (b) There is no interactive audience to provide feedback so that the story writer has difficulty knowing how much detail to provide and about which aspects of the story. I experience this quite often in my writing. Those who have a common social and cultural ancestry (that is, have grown up before the 1960s in Notre Dame Bay, for example) have complained that I provide overly much boring detail. In contrast, some of my readers who hail from Europe and have little intimate knowledge of outport Newfoundland have told me how much they enjoyed the detail and that they have been fascinated by the social and cultural richness that I have conveyed.

Storytelling!

It is an adventure – both to tell stories and to listen.

I love doing both.

It is an honour and a privilege to have become the repository of so many stories of "my people." It is giving me great pleasure to deliver the stories to future generations.

I hope my readers enjoy the stories as much as I do telling them.

I have an apology, of sorts. Some readers have criticized my stories because I have not exercised more "control." That is, I allow the people to tell their stories and I do not exercise any sort of censorship. So, for example, the story of the revival at the Methodist Church at Little Bay Islands is told as Grandmother and my mother related it to me. I have no right to change it to fit someone else's notion of reality. Moreover, there are elements of the supernatural in some of the stories. These elements were in the original rendition of the stories. To leave out these elements is to destroy the stories. Besides, if I dared to do that, where would be the authenticity?

Besides, the purpose of publishing these stories is so that readers will understand the people who are the subject of the stories. Consequently, the stories have to be related according to how they saw their world, how they constructed their reality so that it made sense to them.

That is the way that I demonstrate my pride of and in them and my enormous respect for them. They survived, physically and spiritually where lesser mortals may have succumbed to the vicissitudes of life and the vagaries of geography and climate.

The Boy in the Barrel

Captain Charles Oxford was skipper of the *Masie Ruth*, a
150 foot three-master with twin diesels for supplementary and
emergency power. He had just supervised the off-loading of
a cargo of Labrador salt bulk fish to a broker in the city of
Boston and had now moved the vessel to the docks of East Coast
Exporters in order to receive a full load of general cargo for
his employers, Ralsom Brothers of Exploits, Newfoundland . It is
November 2, 1937.

While the winches were in operation, slinging the lifts of
wooden boxes of dried fruit, crates of glass, bales of this and
sacks of that aboard and down into the three cargo holes in
succession in order to maintain her trim at the dock, a clerk came
down the dock and sprinted over the coaming and straight to the
Captain's cabin.

"Good morning, Captain Oxford, sir, but we have a little
problem."

"A problem? Indeed? Do we now? And, what is the nature of
the problem?"

"It seems, sir, that this vessel is not in the registry of our
insurers. As you are aware, I am sure, sir, it is imperative that
we insure our cargo. This shipment has not been paid for in
advance. We have a long-term business relationship with Ralsom
Brothers and we are happy to extend our services, knowing full

well that in a very short time we will receive payment in full, as per usual. However, although Ralson Brothers, undoubtedly, has the vessel fully insured, usually, such insurance does not extend to cargo owned by a third party unless the owners of the vessel had a declaration that the cargo was fully the property of the vessel's owners, in which case it would be the responsibility of the vessel owners, or the purchasers of the goods, to make insurance arrangements. I gather that you have not already made such arrangements?"

"In fact, young man, you are correct. We have not. What is the procedure, at this time?"

"Well, we will make arrangements with our insurers, but they will need certain legal papers because the vessel is not registered here in the United States. It will be necessary for you to consult with a firm of marine lawyers, a firm that we have had dealings with for a long time. These people will be able to draw up all necessary legal documentations about your vessel and about you as Captain. All formalities, you understand, but necessary, I am afraid, before our insurers will sign on the dotted line. Money calls loudly, sir, money calls loudly."

"Well, by all means, I will pay the firm a visit. Could I not send my first mate? He's my son. He knows as much about this business as I do."

"I don't think so, sir. It has to be Captain, not first officer unless the Captain is disabled or debilitated in some way. I will go and place a telephone call, right away, sir, to the lawyers. I will also arrange a taxi for you. They will be expecting you."

"Thank you. I will come to your office momentarily. Mr. Rowsell, my second mate, is quite able to handle the manifest and supervise the loading."

"The lawyers will need to see your papers, sir. You do, in fact, have papers, do you sir?"

Captain Oxford caught the slightest suggestion of derision. "You are an accountant, are you not?"

"A junior accountant, sir. I am still studying."

"Well, junior accountant, without papers," and Captain Oxford let the studied contempt hang in the air for a few moments, not revealing his amusement of the much too serious and gauchely impertinent young man, "I am an ocean going, fully qualified, fully papered, bona fide, Captain, able to calculate logarithms to determine latitude after fixing my points with my sextant and consulting my book of tables, and able to determine longitude after consulting my chronometer, able to determine a course with compass and parallel rulers on one of his majesty's navigational charts. I can even sing in the choir, read the scriptures, and deliver a sermon in the Methodist church. I have papers. Anything else I can do to provide you with assurance that I can find my way to the office of this lawyer of yours?"

"No sir. I'm sorry sir. I apologize. Please forgive me, sir."

"That's OK young man, we all have some learning to do. I accept your apology."

"Um, excuse me, sir....?"

"Yes?"

"Do you really, I mean, sing in a choir and deliver sermons in the Methodist church?"

"Regularly, young man, regularly. But, now, if you ask me for my papers, I'll have to go in my cabin and bring out my Bible. These are the only papers that qualify me for preaching my sermons to the Lord's faithful or to his supplicants. I don't need your pipsqueak lawyer's signature to deliver a sermon in a House of the Lord." He was laughing.

The young accountant reddened. "Forgive me, sir. I am pleased to meet such a man as yourself. One day, I hope I can deliver a sermon, as well. I believe I may have a call."

"I'm please to hear it, young man. Now, God speed with that telephone call of yours."

"Yes, sir. Thank you, sir." And he turned to go.

"And, young man!"

"Yes sir?"

"You did say that you would arrange a taxi for me?"

"Yes, sir. Of course, sir. That's part of my job. And, sir, if you will not consider me so bold, but in your case, it will be my pleasure."

"Good. I don't often get a chance to call a taxi at Little Bay Islands."

*The Oral and Folk Story Tradition Of Western Notre Dame Bay,
north east coast of Newfoundland Island*

The young man looked at Captain Oxford questioningly. Opened his mouth, but nothing came out. Then, "Thank you, sir, right away sir. And, sir, I've learned a lesson, today. One of humility, sir."

"Don't be overly hard on yourself, young man. If you've learnt a lesson from our little meeting, consider yourself lucky. You didn't have to pay an awful lot for it. Hope that future lessons are no more costly. And, don't be overly prideful of your humility!"

"Thank you, sir. Good day to you. I hope everything goes well for you at the law firm. They specialize in Marine Law, sir. Very proficient." And the young man turned and strode purposefully back to his office.

Captain Oxford took a few minutes to wash his hands and face, comb his graying beard, found his newest Captain's cap and Jersey, kept on his rolled-neck sweater, knitted by his doting wife, took his satchel, and strode up the dock to the already waiting taxi.

****

The offices of Bollingberg House, Grayson & Richard Bollingberg, Marine Lawyers, as the marquee proclaimed in large Gothic letters, was an imposing stone structure of six stories. Captain Oxford reached in his pocket and retrieved some bills with which to pay the cabbie, but was told that the fare had already been paid. The seaman dug in his pockets again, retrieved several pieces of silver coin and handed to the grateful cab driver. He straightened up, turned to go up the steps of the intimidating grand entrance of the building, straightened his cap

46

Tales from Harbour Divine
*The Oral and Folk Story Tradition Of Western Notre Dame Bay,
north east coast of Newfoundland Island*

and said to himself, "OK, let's get this formality nonsense over with and let's get some work done, shall we?"

Inside the building was a large foyer at the back of which, swanked by a large American flag and a number of Marine house flags, presumably those of the shipping and marine firms who paid retainers to this august firm, was a desk behind which was a middle aged woman busy plugging cables into a switchboard.

He waited patiently for a few moments until the lady could attend him.

"Good day, sir. Welcome to Bollingberg House. How may I help you?"

"I'm Captain Charles Oxford of the schooner *Maisie Ruth*. I am to see a lawyer at this establishment."

"Welcome, Captain Oxford. You are expected. The younger Mr. Bollingberg is expecting you. Please approach the lift," and she pointed a finger to where a uniformed elderly black man was standing, "and Mr. Hawkins will take you up the lift and show you to Mr. Bollingbeg's office. I will let them know that you are on the way up"

Having been taken to the top floor and shown the appropriate door, Captain Oxford thanked the lift attendant, tapped on the slightly ajar door, stepped inside and removed his cap, rubbing his left hand through his unruly hair. A pleasant young woman was sitting behind a desk and was engaged in producing some or other document at a large type writing machine. She ceased her clacking. "Captain Oxford, I presume?"

"Charles Oxford, Captain of the *Maise Ruth*, at your service, ma,am." He bowed politely in acknowledgment of her and her question.

The young lady stood, smiled, "Such courtly manners are becoming very rare, Captain Oxford. I am so pleased. Follow me, if you please, Captain."

The young lady led the mariner down a corridor and showed him into a large office with windows from which one had a grand view of Boston Harbour, now full of shipping of every description, even this late in the season. She showed him to a chair in front of a large desk. He sat.

"Shall I pour you a cup of coffee, Captain Oxford? Mr. Bollingberg will be with you shortly."

"Yes, please."

The young lady went swiftly to the back of the office and returned with a large mug of coffee and several cookies on a plate. She placed them on the desk in front of the grizzled mariner.

"He'll be just a few moment, sir."

"Thank you!"

Charles tasted the black coffee. He was amused that she had not offered sugar or milk. Then, he remembered in which country he was.

"Philistines!" he grumbled with a smile, crunched into one of the cookies and sipped the bitter coffee. "How in Heaven's name do they drink this stuff?" he asked himself with a shake of his head.

He continued to sip the coffee as he looked around the very pleasant office. The wall between the windows, behind the desk, was full of framed parchments, a Bachelor of Laws from Harvard University, a Bachelor of Arts from Yale University, and a number of other awards and certificates. The name of the recipient was not as clear as the pre-printed words. He got up to take a closer look. He stared. His knees had suddenly gone to water. The name on the documents was *Richard Osfid Bollingberg*. He shivered, long suppressed memories flooding his being.

"Well, aren't you the big boy. And what is your name, little man?"

"I'm Wichawd Othfid. My daddy's the captain."

"Now, Richard, your daddy's not the captain. He's the second mate."

Captain Garland Ledrew laughed. "Well, I'll tell you, little man, Master Richard Oxford, your dad might not be captain, today, but he's a great second mate and he will be captain one of these days, you mark my words!"

"Me .... I'm goin ta be a captain too. You mawk my woids!"

Captain Ledrew, Richard's mom, his dad - second mate, Charles Oxford- and the other crew of the Rose Marie, laughed delightedly at the precocious little boy.

"And," he said, "Jamesy is goin' ta be a captain, too. But Sheeda can't be a captain 'cause she's a goil. Goil's can't be captain."

There was another round of laughter.

Ledrew, enjoying the conversation, responded, "And who is this Jamsie?"

"Jamsie ith my widdo brudda and Sheeda is my baby thithda. She's preddy."

Everybody laughed at the boys verbosity and his difficulty with pronunciation because of his missing front teeth.

Captain Charles Oxford shook his head to clear away the memories. He stumbled back to his chair.

The young lady returned. "Oh, Captain Oxford, Mr. Bollingberg is going to be another five minutes or so. He apologizes."

"That's OK, young lady, I can wait."

The young woman stared at the man. "Is something wrong, sir?"

"No, no no, I'm, ah I'm fine. It's just a little stuffy in here."

The secretary, assuring herself that the man was not about to have an apoplexy, left the room.

A minute or so later, he looked around the room. On the far wall was a collection of framed photographs. He got up and

50

Tales from Harbour Divine
*The Oral and Folk Story Tradition Of Western Notre Dame Bay,
north east coast of Newfoundland Island*

stepped across to take a look and to kill time while he waited for the lawyer man. He tried not to look at the university diplomas.

He stared! There were photographs of a small boy with his parents, other photos of the boy as he grew older, with his mom, with his dad, with other important-looking men, photos of the man in some sort of black gown, flanked by his obviously proud and pleased mother and father.

Captain Oxford stared at the photo of the boy and the boy as a man. The likeness was uncanny. The photo of the young man with his bride could almost be replaced by his own son, James, now first officer with him on this voyage. What a coincidence! His heart began to race. Hardly able to keep balance, he returned to his chair, sat heavily, and began to sweat. He was about to get up to refill his coffee mug when the door to the side of the room opened and a tall, elderly, white haired man strode in , apologizing profusely.

"I do apologize, Captain Oxford. That meeting took much longer than I had anticipated. I do hope you will forgive me."

Captain Charles Oxford stood.

"I am Grayson Bollingberg, senior partner. I will be looking after your affairs. I am pleased to meet you, Captain Oxford.

"Likewise, sir."

The gentleman held out his hand and firmly shook that of Captain Oxford. Then he moved behind his desk and seated himself in the big leather chair.

"Now, then, Captain Oxford, I have already received a call from East Coast Exporters, so we will be able to settle this little business with dispatch."

The gentleman, at least seventy, according to Captain Oxford's assessment, pulled out several drawers of his desk and selected a variety of papers. He picked up the telephone and asked for Miss. Heathton. The young lady who had greeted Captain Oxford at the office entered the room and was requested to retrieve some additional forms. She left and returned moments later with a cardboard file stuffed with papers.

In the meantime, Mr. Bollingberg was keeping a conversation going.

"Where do you hail from, Captain Oxford?"

"I live in the village of Little Bay Islands, sir, on the north east coast of Newfoundland."

"Oh, yes, Newfoundland. We do business with several Newfoundland based shipping firms every year, as many as a dozen, some years."

Mr. Bollingberg opened the file and selected some papers. "Now, then, Captain Oxford, the name of your vessel is ....?"

Captain Oxford opened his satchel and handed some papers across the desk. "Registration papers, sir, the *Maisie Ruth*, registered at St. John's Newfoundland, owned by Ralson Brothers of Exploits, Newfoundland."

The elderly gentleman hummed to himself as he transcribed the necessary information. "A hundred and fifty feet, eh. What's she like in rough weather?"

"She's a beauty, sir, handles fine. But we have supplementary power, twin diesels, which we engage as necessary. One is always running at low speed for electricity for our running lights. We also have kerosene running lights in case the electricity fails for some reason."

"Lifeboats, Captain Oxford?"

"Four sir, according to regulations. Inspected annually, each containing rations, tarps, water, and compass."

"Now, then Captain Oxford. Who is your first and second officers?"

"First officer, first mate's ticket, is my son, James Oxford, age 28." Second officer, but also with first mate's ticket is Cranford Rowsell, age 29."

"Very good. Now then, Captain Oxford, we have to get personal. I need your vitals. Place of birth, date of birth, and so on."

"Little Bay Islands, June 14, 1883. I am fifty four years old."

"Could I see your certificates, please, your tickets?"

"Captain Oxford selected more papers from his case and handed them across the table."

"Now, then, Captain Oxford, your marine record. Aw, I see ... ummm ... You have had a lot of experience, Captain Oxford."

"Yes, I have, sir, started when I was 15 years old as a fisherman on the Labrador."

The elderly gentleman across the desk was staring at Charles. He looked back at the papers and looked up again. His jaws were working as if trying to formulate a comment or question. He stopped, looked back at the papers. He took a deep breath, seemed agitated.

"Captain Oxford, ah, it says, here, that you served on the," he paused, "the *Marie Rose*, registered at St. John's, Newfoundland."

"Yes, I did.'

"For how long?"

"I believe my papers say from May 14, 1909 to November 7, 1912."

"Yes, that is correct, according to your papers."

"Is something wrong?"

The man took a deep breath. "No, Captain Oxford, nothing is wrong with your information. But, why don't we take a break. I need to gather some information."

Mr. Bollingberg picked up the telephone: "Miss. Heathton, call Richard at Sampson and Collins and tell him to return immediately. This is an emergency. We have a situation. Immediately, you understand. Now!" He barked the last words.

Bollingberg turned to Captain Oxford, raised his eyebrows, forced a smile, "If you want action, you gotta yell, sometimes. My son and partner, Richard, is across the street, consulting with another firm. He'll be along momentarily. May I get a refill for your coffee?"

Captain Charles Oxford was not a mere naïve marine rating. He had dealt with many men and from all walks of life. He was not being fooled. He knew something was afoot. There seemed to be something wrong with his papers, although he couldn't imagine what."

Bollingberg returned with the coffee and tried chatting, but he was clearly agitated or excited, almost as if he was thinking he had captured some wanted criminal or something, stalling Charles, waiting for the police, or something. "Ah, Captain Oxford, how long will it take you to get back to home port?"

"With fair winds, sir, we could do it in five days, easy, if we didn't have to make any other ports of call. It's approximately a thousand miles, give or take a handful. We can do eight knots with a full cargo and a fair wind. With an officer and a crewman always on watch, we need not stop at all, depending, of course, on wind and wave conditions. Fortunately, at this time of year, unlike in the spring, we don't have to worry about floating ice, and it's a bit early for ice to form on the vessel.

Of course, we watch the glass. If the pressure is dropping, then we make for the nearest port. We consider our voyage in segments. Boston to Halifax, about 400 nautical miles; Halifax to St, John's, about 500; St John's to Exploits on a curve, if we take the offshore route, is about 200, give or take. Now, on this voyage, I have some cargo for St. John's so it will be an additional day or two for our transactions there. So, from the day of leaving Boston harbour, we could be back in Exploits inside a week. Then, I take my own small motor boat and make the couple of hours run across the bay to my home at Little Bay Islands.

The older man was obviously grateful that Captain Oxford had so conveniently filled the time. He was about to say something when a young man, thirtyish, burst into the office without knocking.

"What is it, Father?" He stopped, looked at Charles. "Oh, excuse me." He looked at the elder Bollingberg. "Did I interrupt something?"

The elder Bollingberg spoke, "No, my son, you didn't. This is Captain Charles Oxford. Captain Oxford, this is my son and partner, Richard Bollingberg."

The young man offered Charles his hand as Charles Oxford stood.

Captain Oxford stared. The young man stared. His mouth fell open. Both men seized control of their responses, released their grip, but remained staring at each other. The elder Bollingberg sat heavily in his chair and was staring at both men.

"Richard!"

That broke the spell.

"Come here, my son, and look at this."

The younger Bollingberg hastened around the desk and looked at Oxford's papers. He looked up at Charles.

"Captain Oxford, it says, here, that you served on the *Marie Rose.*"

"Yes."

"Can you tell us about that?"

"The *Marie Rose* was lost at sea." He was looking at the Bollingberg men, flint in his eyes. He was daring them to contradict him.

Richard sat in a chair just to the side of his father, "Captain Oxford, were you on the *Marie Rose* when she was lost?"

"Yes ...... I was."

"Were there any other survivors?"

"No!"

"Would you tell us what happened, please?"

"No! It is no longer important! There was an inquiry. I took the stand at the Supreme Court at St. John's in the summer of 1913. I told my story. It's all on the record. You can get it there. I don't see how that has anything to do with insurance."

"It doesn't have anything whatever to do with the insurance, Captain Oxford. But, I have an interest in such things. I am requesting that you tell me the story. Please, sir!" There was intense suppressed emotion in the younger man's voice.

Tales from Harbour Divine
The Oral and Folk Story Tradition Of Western Notre Dame Bay,
north east coast of Newfoundland Island

57

Oxford took a deep breath, fighting back memories. "It is a sad story, sir. I don't mean to offend. But I would find it very difficult,"

"And, if I insist?"

"It is painful, sir, even to listen to. You don't want to hear it."

"I do, indeed, want to hear the story, Mr. Oxford. Maybe, if I showed you something ....."

Richard took a folder that his father had fished out of a drawer. He opened it and riffled through the mostly newspaper clippings. He took one and passed to Charles.

It was the front page of the _Boston Tribune_, dated Monday, November 18, 1912.

Late item: SHIP LOST AT SEA: We have received a report that a vessel by the name of _Marie Rose_ has been lost at sea. There seems to have been only one survivor. We hope to have a full story in tomorrow's edition.

Captain Charles Oxford stared at the faded newspaper page. He shivered. He fought for control of his emotions. He reached for his cup. It was empty. The elder Bollingberg quickly got up and went to the back of the room and returned with a fresh cup of coffee. Nobody said anything.

With enormous control and speaking very slowly and in a monotone, Captain Oxford began his narration: "I came into the world in 1883. I was fifteen years old when I first went to the Labrador with my father, summer 1888. I was given a special position because Mr. Wallace Strong thought that I would make

58

Tales from Harbour Divine
*The Oral and Folk Story Tradition Of Western Notre Dame Bay,
north east coast of Newfoundland Island*

a good officer on one of his vessels, so he decided to give me early experience. Grandfather Oxford had been my teacher and I was good at reading and writing and ciphering, as they called mathematics in those days. I already knew logarithms and trigonometry.

By May 1909, when I was just 26 years old I was second mate on the newly built *Marie Rose*. We had just returned from the Labrador in October 1912, and Mr. Wallace Strong, of Strong Brothers of Little Bay Islands, asked me if I would like to go to St. John's with the load of fish and to pick up some cargo. He said that I could take Melissa, my wife, and Richard, our five year old son. We left our three year old boy, James, and our infant daughter, Sheila, in care of Melissa's younger sister, Melinda Locke, and her parents. Melissa and Richard were so excited. Melissa had never been south of Notre Dame Bay and little Richard was excited because he thought he was going to be the captain. He was a great favourite of the crew because he used to talk non-stop and had difficulty with his pronunciation because he had lost his front teeth.

We had a good voyage to St, John's, offloaded and loaded again and left St. John's November 5 in the morning, a pet day, clear sunny sky.

We were half way across Conception Bay, keeping well out, when the sky rapidly clouded over and it began to snow. By the time we were off Baccalieu the wind had come up from the westard, so Captain Ledrew said that we would try to make in to Bay de Verde or Old Perlican.   But we were not able to tack against the wind. The Captain decided to take the ship off shore a ways and to try to come about and come in to the shelter of Baccalieu Island and, maybe, to get into Bay de Verde or maybe further in the bay, maybe Harbour Grace. But, the winds came up much stronger, and we were in a raging blizzard by nightfall.

We battled the storm all night. My wife was sick, but little Richard thought that it was all a lot of fun. He was being a captain, he said.

Next day, the winds were screaming overhead and we were being tossed about. We lost our after spar, first, then our for'ward one.

LeDrew came to me and said that we were lost and if I wanted to save my son, I should put him in a puncheon and toss him overboard. Oh, sir, I didn't want to do that. But, as the elements screamed above us. Melissa told me to do as Captain LeDrew said. We, she said, would not survive, but maybe little Richard might have a chance.

So, gentlemen, I talked to him, to Richard, told him that he was going to be a captain. I nailed some chain - for ballast, you see ... " He looked up at the two men, but quickly dropped his eyes ... " to ah, to ... the inside of the puncheon opposite to the bung hole and put Richard in with a lot of blankets, some food, something to plug the bunghole if water started to come in, and I made a small flag to poke up through the bung hole if he felt the barrel hit something.

After I headed up the barrel, sir, he began to cry. I knew he was frightened. I began to cry, as well."

60

Tales from Harbour Divine
The Oral and Folk Story Tradition Of Western Notre Dame Bay,
north east coast of Newfoundland Island

Captain Oxford was now sobbing. The elder Bollingberg handed him an handkerchief. It was some moments before he could continue.

"I saw a can of paint there in the cargo hole. I beat it open and with a piece of rope I painted *Marie Rose* on the top of the Puncheon and then I painted St. Johns, NFLD on the bottom. Richard was crying and asking to be released. I was not able to continue. Ledrew sent two men down in the hold and tied some rope around the puncheon and drew it on deck and threw it overboard. The ship was breaking up. We all knew that it was all over.

It was almost dark when Captain Ledrew said to take to the lifeboats. I managed to get Melissa into one lifeboat and cut it away and jumped in. Two other sailors also got a boat cut away and managed to get in it. I saw LeDrew jump for the boat but I don't think he made it. The vessel was breaking up before our eyes, pummeled by the seas. I don't know what happen to the other three hands: Robert Hewlett from Long Island, Charlie Bridger from Dark Tickles and Michael Kelly from Fogo Island. I guess they either went down with the boat or managed to get in a life boat. They were never seen again.

Well, the boat that Melissa and I were in drifted and, I guess, I fell asleep. We were wet and cold.

Next thing I know I was in bed. The people told me that I was in the home of a Glavine family in Bay Bulls - that's the south east coast of the island, below St. John's - and that I had been found almost frozen to death. I asked about my wife and they told me that I was found embracing my wife but that she had already died. Patrick Caravan, in the other boat, was also rescued and was able to tell what happened, but he died next day. I am the only survivor. I don't know how the Boston newspaper knew about that. I guess there must have been a cable from St. John's.

I was eventually taken by boat to St. John's and was in hospital for almost two months because of the frostbite."

He pulled up the sleeve of his jacket and then his shirt and showed some of the damaged flesh. Then, he pulled up both trouser legs and showed his ugly legs, damaged all those years ago by the unrelenting frosts.

"I go back to Bay Bulls every year or two to visit the Glavines, a wonderful gentle Roman Catholic family. The old folk are getting up in years now, and finding it difficult. I am able to help them a bit. It's the least I can do.

After a year, I married Melissa's sister, Melinda. She was a wonderful mother to James and Sheila. We have four more children. She is a wonderful woman.

James has become a professional seaman just as our little Richard predicted. He is now first officer with me on this voyage.

So, gentlemen, now you know my story. I lost my wife and my son. I don't know what else to say."

The elder gentleman handed him another newspaper clipping. It told of a fisherman finding a small boy in a barrel, barely alive.

The article included this information:

62

Tales from Harbour Divine
*The Oral and Folk Story Tradition Of Western Notre Dame Bay,
north east coast of Newfoundland Island*

The one survivor of the ill-fated *Marie Rose,* whose tragic loss at sea was reported in yesterday's paper, is a small boy. He was found in a barrel by a fisherman out from Jonestown.

The boy says that his name is Richard Othfid and that he has a little brother, Jamsie, who is going to be a captain and that he has a sister, Sheeda.

The boy speaks English but with a British or Irish accent. He knows his letters, his numbers, his colours, and can even read simple words. It is believed the lost ship is British.

It is an old custom to place children in barrels if a ship is in imminent danger of sinking.

Charles Oxford looked up in disbelief. "My son? My son was saved? Thanks be to God! But, what happened to him? I wonder if he can forgive me? I wonder if he would want to see me?

The elder lawyer said nothing. He looked at Richard. The young man nodded assent. The elder Bollingburg handed Charles another clipping, dated December 16, 1912:

"The boy rescued from the barrel from the *Marie Rose* has been adopted by a prominent Boston family whose name is not being revealed. However, authorities have declared that this may be an interim adoption pending the discovery of some information about the boy's family."

Charles looked up. The younger Bollingberg was standing. "Mr. Oxford, I have something to show you. I have a storage room down at the lower level. I keep some very important things there. Come with me please." He looked at his father. The latter gentleman shook his head indicating that only the younger man should accompany Captain Oxford.

The Oral and Folk Story Tradition Of Western Notre Dame Bay,
north east coast of Newfoundland Island

The two men waited for the lift. They went down in silence. Through a long dimly-lit corridor they proceeded to a door at the end. Richard fumbled with keys until he found the right one. He opened the door and switched on a light. There were numerous shelves full of boxes and to the side a large object shrouded with a sheet.

Captain Charles Oxford shivered as Richard went over to the object and pulled off the sheet. There was an old puncheon, with *Marie Rose*, in white straggly letters. The other letters had obviously been washed away by the ocean.

Charles dropped to his knees and began to sob.

"Oh, will he ever forgive me, will he ever forgive me?"

"Oh, I think he will forgive you."

"Captain Oxford, please stand up."

"Father, I am Richard. I am your son."

The two men, now both sobbing uncontrollably, embraced.

++++++++

Over dinner, Richard met his brother, the Jamsie whom he still remembered as his little brother. Richard said that he could still remember the harbour where he was a child, even though he had no idea where it was. He said that he remembered many schooners at anchor in that harbour. He had no recollection of the storm or of being in the barrel.

+++++++

In July, 1938, Richard Oxford Bollingberg, accompanied by his wife and two children, visited Little Bay Islands and stayed for two weeks, met his little sister, Sheila, now 28 years old with three children of her own, and renewed his acquaintance with his forgotten relatives, which included about three quarters of the people of the village. He visited the old Methodist church, the one built under the supervision of his grandfather back in the late 1800s, and visited his mother's grave. On the Sunday before he left, he and his family attended a thanksgiving service led by the lay-reader. He, now being Jewish, the religion of his adoptive family, was given the privilege of reading from his Torah which he always carried with him.

Richard and his family visited Newfoundland many times since then, even after his father died and he was an elderly man. He always attended service at the Methodist church with James and their collective families and was always invited to read scripture. Richard insisted that his children, although Jewish, learn about Christianity so that they would have a greater appreciation of their Newfoundland relatives.

Captain Charles Oxford died in 1960 at age 81. Richard died at Boston in July, 1998 at age 91.

The End

William Ryan's Strange Encounter

Almost everybody in Western Notre Dame Bay knows about the cave on the far southern end of Long Island, there on Sudder Head just above the Follies. That's the cave which the renown anthropologist, Ingeborg Marshall, excavated numerous Aboriginal artifacts. Although the cave is difficult to access, requiring some scrambling up over almost sheer cliff, there is sufficient evidence to indicate that people have been regularly visiting the cave for thousands of years. Just why the Aboriginals utilized that cave for their interment rituals is a matter of mythical speculation. The cave is of such anthropological importance that several local government and tourist groups are advocating that a road be constructed so that tourists can have easy access.

The cave is not well hidden, even if it is a little difficult to access. If one stands off the land - in a boat, of course - a half kilometer or so, there it is, in all of its dark and mysterious grandeur, just visible through the fog. Maybe, because it was visible and yet relatively accessible, it has served multiple purposes over the years.

There are stories of young couples, seeking seclusion for amorous purposes, making use of the cave, after a rowboat ride from Cutwell Arm or even from Dark Tickles. Fishermen have used it as shelter if they happened to be caught overnight with a storm welling up. Boys have used it since there were boys living on Long Island and on neighbouring islands, at least since around 1650 for boys of European ancestry and, no doubt, boys of the Beothuck. Dorset and earlier cultures from time immemorial. Still do, in fact. Boys will be boys.

All of this is well known. What seems to have been generally forgotten, now, is that the cave also served another purpose. Some time in the mid to late 1700s, say 1775 give or take five or ten years, an interesting event occurred at this particular cave.

On one early autumn day before their fathers had returned from fishing on the Labrador, and early in the morning when their mothers weren't looking, three bedlamer lads from Cutwell Arm swiped bread from their respective mother's pantries, rounders - small dried codfish, gutted but not deboned - from their fathers' stages, scrambled aboard a small rowboat and went for a ride. They headed north east out of "the Arm," then south east and then east towards the cave that they had seen from off shore but had not yet visited. They landed on the rocks, tied the punt on to a standin' stalligan on the shore, and scrambled up over the scree and cliff to the cave.

At first, on their accessing the cave, the boys were a little disappointed. It was just a cave with a dirt floor, liberally sprinkled with rocks, stones, dried wood, and the remains of numerous camp fires. Deciding to stay awhile they proceeded to build a fire over which to toast their bit of bread and roast their rounders. When the fire was going full blazes, they looked around for additional fuel. In process of retrieving a piece of wood that had lain on the cave floor for many years, some of the dirt was overturned and a shiny object was exposed: a belt buckle of most curious design. Although the boys had never actually seen much silver except, maybe, the odd silver coin, they knew immediately that the ornate belt buckle could be nothing else but solid silver, carefully made, richly engraved. They looked at teach other, beaming. The search was on!.

Where there is one thing, there might be another. With a whoop and a holler, toast forgotten, the boys began to dig with their bare hands into the dirt and stones of the cave floor. At first, they were disappointed. All they uncovered was the almost completely disintegrated leather belt to which the buckle likely belonged. But, while pulling the old leather out of the earth, it broke. Why would it break?

They began to dig some more and soon discovered the remainder of the belt to which was attached a silver band to which was attached a silver chain, each of the links being about a half inch long. They pulled on the chain, but it was attached to still something else. They had dug as far as they could with their hands and had to resort to moving some fairly large stones with long pieces of wood. Finally, at the end of about eighteen inches of chain they discovered a long round object, a cylinder about an inch in diameter and ten or so inches long, also made of what was obviously pure silver, also richly engraved, containing the arms of some old European family and words that they though might have been Spanish. In fact, the script might have been in almost any language other than their version of contemporary English.

It didn't take them long to determine how to disengage the latch on the top of the cylinder and excitedly retrieve a rancid roll of cloth. They carefully unrolled the cloth and discovered a tight roll of heavily oiled, very thin, leather. They unrolled the leather, amazed at what was contained in the leather roll - a piece of parchment with a map. Although the inks were a little dull, the map was still quite easy to read. With heads together they turned the map every which way until, orienting it according to the arrow on the map, they realized that the map was of Long Island, although maybe not accurately drawn. There seemed to be no doubt to the boys that they had stumbled on a map showing the location of a trove of pirate treasure. The X seemed to be indicating a small pond on the north end of the island. Although they had, each, circumnavigated Long Island on several occasions, they had not known of the existence of that pond, a mile or so to the east of the village of Lushes Bight.

Exactly what happened during the next few minutes has never been quite determined. It may have been a genuine accident. It appears that Philip Closter grabbed the map from the hands of Charles Simmonds and that Timothy Thevin tried to grab it away from Philip. In the melee, Charles Simmonds succeeded in grabbing the map again, but tripped and fell into the fire. The oiled leather and the parchment flashed into flame as did Charles' clothing. Before either of the boys could react, so they said afterward, Charles bolted for the cave opening and attempted to jump into the ocean, about forty feet below, but didn't reach his objective. He might have made it except for the unfortunate fact that the ocean was at low tide. Charles landed on the rocks, still afire, and died - instantly, the other two boys said. The map was thoroughly consumed by the flames.

Although the two boys stuck to their story, and gave the chain and silver tube to Charles' mother, suspicion surrounded them and their families. When the fisher fathers arrived home from the Labrador in late October, the invective and accusations grew to dangerous proportions, so much so that Michael Simmonds, Charles' father declared that he would murder Philip and Timothy for their having murdered his son.

Wisely, within weeks, and before the ocean began to freeze, the Thevin and Closter families hired a schooner to take them south across the bay. Just where they went, nobody could say. Even though the mothers of both families left siblings in and around Cutwell Arm, this was not a period in history when people were literate. Without the abilities to read and write, there was very little communication. In short, they were never heard of or from again.

Strangely, some said with a broken heart, others said of grief, some said of contrariness, others declared suicide, Michael Simmonds died suddenly just after Christmas, leaving his wife, Salona, with three small children: two pre-teen daughters and a smaller son.

Through the good graces of the Church of England minister, Salona became aware of a young widowed fisherman across the bay at Western Arm, and he of her. As soon as shipping opened up in April, Salona and her children were fetched by a schooner from the north side of Green Bay and she married the fisherman from Western Arm. Thus, she passed out of the history, myth

70

Tales from Harbour Divine
*The Oral and Folk Story Tradition Of Western Notre Dame Bay,
north east coast of Newfoundland Island*

and lore of Long Island. It would be a hundred or so years later before Salona Simmonds' name would again be mentioned on Long Island.

Although Salona and her family had left Cutwell Arm, and although the Thevin and Closter families had moved on to parts unknown, and although even the names of the families became foggy in memory and eventually lost altogether on Long Island, the story continued to live. As soon as the story of the presumed "treasure map" got across the island from the south end at Cutwell Arm to the north end of Lushes Bight, a distance of a mere three miles, there were those at the latter village who felt vindicated.

On numerous occasions, people – men and boys – from Lushes Bight had had strange experiences at Kelly Cove and at Kelly Cove Pond. Choruses of, "I told you so" followed by renewed interest in stories that had been told about Kelly Cove and vicinity for several generations: strange meetings, stories that made the hair on your back to raise, ghostly apparitions, unearthly sounds that made ones blood run cold, meetings with men dressed in costumes of a by-gone era who told them "thou shalt not pass" when they went too near the pond; fishing rooms mysteriously torn down when some of the livyers thought to build stages and wharves a little closer to the fishing grounds.

Some of the older boys, poo-pooing the superstitions of their elders, had ventured to build camps near the pond. All went well until they dared to spend a night in these impertinent, even if crude, structures. The boys said that they never heard such unholy screeches and bangings on the outside of their camps. They thought that the devil himself was about to grab them. Frightened to stay, but equally afraid to go outside in the darkness, they shivered in fear the whole night long, lighting candle after candle, afraid to let the cabin go dark, shitting in their pants in their terror, and ashamed to return to Lushes Bight in the morning. Returning with their fathers later in the day to retrieve some of their abandoned belongings, they discovered their camps destroyed, boards and other paraphernalia scattered around.

The story repeated itself from generation to generation from the late sixteen hundreds, when the first European settlers had arrived in the area, until the eighteen forties. Each succeeding generation of boys would call the bluff of their ancestors, believing that, for some unknown reason, their elders were frightening them away from the area even while they suggested alternate possible sites for the boys' camps, the events played themselves out generation after generation with unfailing regularity.

Although none of it made sense to rational people - and if nothing else, these people prided themselves on their rationality - the inexplicable happenings were sufficient that even as late as 1860, nobody ventured to lay a claim to or to build any kind of structure - let alone a dwelling house - near either Kelly Cove beach or Kelly Cove Pond.

And, ordinarily, that's where the story would have ended. A ghost story of indeterminate source, almost, with some people frightened out of their wits, all happening a long time ago with details forgotten or lost in the mists of the past, especially in the absence of recorded history. The story would have been related by an older person, ridiculed as foolishness, and dismissed. That's what always happens.

About fifty years after the adventures of the three boys at that cave, another squalling brat, another mouth to feed with too few potatoes, another male child was born to another poor farmer of the Ryan clan in the village of Callan, County Kilkenny, Ireland. William Ryan was born midsummer, 1821.

The once-proud Ryan clan, able to trace its ancestry back as far as AD 144, descendent from the Spanish King Milesius and Fiacha Baiceada, son of Cathire More, King of Ireland, and able to enumerate many warriors, bards and learned men of Irish history, once Lords of Idrone and Owney and owning most of Carlow and Leinster, were now in reduced circumstances. Ancestral lands had been divided and subdivided and finally were seized by the British crown and passed over as a gift to the likes of some or other ass-liking English Baron or Viscount. The destitute Ryan Clan in and around Callan had little choice but to immigrate. Immigrate or starve.

Many of that family went to the United States, some to Australia and New Zealand, others to Canada, and a shipload of brothers and cousins arrived in Twillingate, Newfoundland in the early summer of 1830, still repeating to each other how they should be proud to be Black Irish, having the additional Spanish ancestry attributed to the sailors shipwrecked on the coast of Ireland when the great Armada of Philip II was destroyed by the *divine wind* in 1588. These sailors, Catholic and Moorish, were adopted into the various clans and their genetic contribution

Tales from Harbour Divine
*The Oral and Folk Story Tradition Of Western Notre Dame Bay,
north east coast of Newfoundland Island*

73

produced a variant in the Irish population, no longer blond and rudy, but dark and black haired.

These newly arrived immigrants to Newfoundland also repeated the ancient family motto, *Malo More Quam Foedari*, which is variously translated as, "I would rather die than be unfaithful," or "I would rather die than be disgraced," or "Death before dishonour," and various other similar translations. These poor Irishmen persisted in perceiving themselves as honourable people, whose word was their bond, whose vow meant that their life was on the line, a promise made was a promise kept. They lived in horror that they might be perceived to cheat, to be fearful, to not do what they said they would do. It meant that they carried the ethos and ethic of integrity to extremes, even when it mean that the results were unnecessarily detrimental to themselves. It was and still is a sentiment that defined them, even if, today, some of the clan, with little education or knowledge of family history, might honour the venerable motto more in the breach than in adherence.

Having arrived safely at Twillingate and after a quick service of thanksgiving there on the strand, with a veritable blizzard of Hail Mary's - probably the first ever- maybe the only - Roman Catholic service on Twillingate Island, these men and their sons dispersed. Some of them went to Pilley's Island, others to St. Brendan's Island and Kings Cove, virtually all becoming fishermen. Michael Ryan moved to Bonavista and opened a public house. Michael's son, John, started a business at Bonavista that lasted until well into the mid-1900s.

74

Tales from Harbour Divine
The Oral and Folk Story Tradition Of Western Notre Dame Bay,
north east coast of Newfoundland Island

Young William, barely nine years old, went to Pilley's Island with his father. When he was sixteen years old, late autumn, 1837, William sailed to St. John's as a deckhand on a schooner transporting a cargo of dried cod. Rather than returning to Pilley's Island, he took a job as deckhand with Captain Michael Fitzgerald of Bay Bulls. Two year's later, 1839, William married Captain Fitzgerald's seventeen year old daughter, Martha, and the young couple moved to St. Mary's, on the Southern Shore, to represent Captain Fitzgerald's growing fish-exporting business. The following year, William's beloved Martha died in childbirth.

The now-twenty year old William made his way back to Pilley's Island, intending to follow his father to the Labrador fishery. Hearing of a likely wife, Sarah Burton (nee, Heath), widow of Youngie, at Cutwell Arm, William paid the young woman a visit, married her, adopted her children, Esther Ann and Youngie, and set up housekeeping with Sarah in her home at Cutwell Arm. It was now 1841.

After several other children were born to the couple, another William – called by his descendants, William II – saw the light of day at Cutwell Arm on May 6, 1849. William II quickly gained the reputation of being much like his father, afraid of nothing, prepared to take on the devil himself, any time, anywhere, the family motto forever on his lips. The ancient family motto defined him.

The local people both cherished and loathed him: to obtain his bond meant a friend for life; to cross him meant that one was to live in dread until he had his vengeance. He respected nobody more than himself, and many a good deal less. If one suggested, when he accompanied his father to the Labrador fishery, that William was not doing his share or was late to be abed or exerting less effort than another man in any way was to invite a challenge. The offended William would not - could not - back down. To do so was tantamount to cowardice. Better to die than be so disgraced. One or the other would apologize or fight or die.

William would never rest until the insult was answered. If the rash offender did not apologize then there was no remedy other than a fight. William was prepared to fight, and if he fought it would be to his own death or to the death of the offender or until the opponent pled mercy. William had no back doors. William was straight up. If one asked William's opinion, then William looked the person straight in the eye and responded. If the person didn't like William's opinion, then it was a lesson not to ask William's opinion if one was not prepared to accept the response.

On the other hand, nobody ever knew William to seek a confrontation, never with aforethought insulted another man. He would, however, accost a man who, in his opinion, was not keeping up his end of the task of fishing, and he was prepared to back up his assessment, with his fists as necessary. He asked much less from others than he saw himself giving. His father was proud of him. Despite his Labrador aboriginal ancestry, through his mother, William II was an Irish Ryan, Irish Catholic, a Black Irish through and through.

Both Williams absorbed the lore of Cutwell Arm and area and knew of the events of the previous century and of the cave. They also knew of the hauntings at the other end of the island and laughed them off as the superstitions and childish terrors of

76

Tales from Harbour Divine
The Oral and Folk Story Tradition Of Western Notre Dame Bay,
north east coast of Newfoundland Island

the Protestants, the latter not having access to the good Catholic confessional to rid them of their load of guilt and shame.

William II took his time to select a wife, having his eye on a girl of the Croucher Clan of Cutwell Arm, the pretty Amelia. But, she was still a bit young. He bided his time.

In the meantime, land already at a premium on both ends of Long Island, William II applied for and obtained a government grant to Kelly Cove, four acres. The local people, at both ends of the island, approached the young man and advised him to repent of his folly. William was not the sort of man to repent a decision. While waiting for Amelia Croucher to be old enough to ask for her hand in marriage, William worked non-stop building a house and premises at Kelly Cove.

Even during the construction phase of William's Kelly Cove premises, strange and unusual events transpired. Somebody broke off William's six foot long pit saw. He swore on the damned Protestants at Lushes Bight. Somebody else turned over a box of cut nails and trampled them in the mud. He swore on the damned Arangemen. Somebody cast aside the main supports of the walkway from the shore to his stage; somebody broke a full box of window glazing.

William was livid! He cursed the Protestants of Lushes Bight who, he was sure, were interfering because they didn't want a Roman Catholic living so close to their village. William purchased new glazing; he continued to build, daring anyone, any thing (!!) to show themselves or itself while he was at his work. He cursed the devil! He shouted at Lucifer! He challenged the demons! He was not afraid! He challenged the devil to combat. He was afraid of nothing!

When William turned age 23, Amelia was 17. The maiden had waited for William's proposal and had spurned all others, William and Amelia were married in the Methodist Church at Cutwell Arm, May, 1872. The happy couple immediately moved to their new home at Kelly Cove. Amelia was delighted with the spacious and well-appointed home and looked forward to setting up a vegetable garden in several promising spots. Nearby, Kelly Cove Pond was a ready source of water even in the driest months. The young couple spent only a couple of nights there together, however, because William left for the Labrador fishery less than a fortnight afterwards. Amelia moved back with her mother at Cutwell Arm for the summer.

William returned home in mid-October and he and Amelia returned to their new home at Kelly Cove.

Problems started almost immediately.

The girl was frightened out of her wits at a loud knocking at their door one snowy November night. William got out of bed, went downstairs in his swanskins and opened the porch door. Nobody was there. There were no tracks in the snow. But, there, off in the shadows of the garden ... Was that a man? A man dressed all in black? One of the bastard Protestants from Lushes Bight wanting to frighten him away, no doubt.

The next night it happened again.

This time, however, William was ready. He raced down stairs without any candle, almost breaking his neck in the process. His

78

Tales from Harbour Divine
The Oral and Folk Story Tradition Of Western Notre Dame Bay, north east coast of Newfoundland Island

loaded muzzle loader was leaning against the facing of the porch door. He quickly fitted the percussion cap, opened the door. No body there. No tracks. There, in the gloom of the trees, a man! He put his gun to his shoulder and fired. He knew his aim was good. He closed the door, grimly satisfied, knowing that in the morning he would have to content with a batch of bastard Protestants from Lushes Bight because he had shot one of their own, one of their Orangemen, doubtlessly.

Nothing happened! No irate villagers came seeking his head or his balls. Nothing! He was astounded, puzzled, mystified.

Throughout the winter, the young couple, even though delighted with their home and the solitude, pleased themselves by taking walks in the snow, building fires in the woods, enjoying each other's company. They also continued to have unusual experiences: banging at the door, knocking at their windows, raking down the strakes of the clapboard, and bloodcurdling screeches, all in the middle of the night, none of which left any tracks or other signs in the snow.

Amelia became fearful, would hardly let William out of her sight. If they were outside and if she needed to go to the outdoor toilet, William had to stand guard. If William walked to Lushes Bight to go to the general store, Amelia went along as well, the trek becoming increasingly difficult for her in her now advanced pregnancy.

Mid-February came. A time of myth-engendering winter blizzards and snow almost up to the second floor windows at the back of the house. Amelia's labour began. Although Amelia's

The Oral and Folk Story Tradition Of Western Notre Dame Bay, north east coast of Newfoundland Island

mother had been staying with the young couple for the past several weeks, Mrs. Croucher had already made it known to Virtue Parsons, the midwife at Lushes Bight, that she would be called on when the time came.

Early morning on February 20, Friday, found Virtue Parsons following along behind William as both, on snowshoes, made the trek, through the swirling snow and screeching winds, along the winding trail from Lushes Bight to Kelly Cove.

As was perfectly normal, Amelia waited for the real birth pangs to begin. In the meantime she was being pampered by the two older women there in the parlour where William had moved their bed about a month previously, for just this occasion. William kept the fire going and the house toasty warm. The storm continued to rage. One could hardly see the woodhouse through the driving snow, the latter structure barely fifty feet away to the side of the dwelling house.

They all had a hearty supper, cooked by Mrs. Croucher, and were gossiping, as is appropriate under the circumstances. About nine of the pendulum clock on the mantle above the fireplace, Amelia's pangs began in earnest. As she bellowed in pain, screeching responses echoed through the blizzard. The two older women looked at each other. Again Amelia cried out in pain; again the screeching above the storm. Although neither of the women were Catholic, they both made the sign of the cross over themselves and Amelia.

Both women were to relate, later, that they had never been so afraid before in their lives, that the screeches coming from the storm were surely from the devil himself.

80

Tales from Harbour Divine
The Oral and Folk Story Tradition Of Western Notre Dame Bay,
north east coast of Newfoundland Island

The birth seemed to be going fine. Mrs. Croucher had seen many births; Mrs. Parsons had attended to more than a hundred. Nothing was unusual.

With a cry from Amelia that almost shattered eardrums, a cry the likes of which neither woman had ever heard before, Amelia fell back on her pillow. Another unearthly screech echoed from the blizzard.

Amelia was dead!

The baby was dead!

Mrs. Croucher began to wail.

Mrs. Parsons drew the cover up over Amelia face and closed the staring lifeless eyes. She hurried to the kitchen to inform the young expectant father. He rushed out doors and bellowed his curses at the winds. Mrs. Parsons reported that she was sure that the winds answered back, a gloating screech, the likes of which she never wanted to hear again. She said it sounded as if the blizzard was expressing its satisfaction and delight over the death of the comely young woman.

A few days later, when the men of the village were able to shovel away the snow and hack a grave through the frozen earth, Amelia Ryan and her unborn baby were laid to rest in the Methodist cemetery at Cutwell Arm.

Immediately after the funeral an embittered William returned directly to Kelly Cove, walking the four miles alone, spurning his father's offer to accompany him.

William spent the remainder of the winter nights alone at Kelly Cove, but walking to Cutwell Arm every morning to help his father prepare for the coming fishing season. He walked home to Kelly Cove every evening after dark. He never mentioned hearing or seeing anything unusual.

It was only decades later, when he was an old widower, living with his son at Roberts Arm, that he admitted that the sounds in the night, when he was there by himself, were enough to curdle his blood. He was convinced, at least at that time, or at least he convinced himself, that there must have been some formation of rocks or some formation of trees or some similar combination that produced the weird sound effects when the wind was a certain way.

William never, not for a moment, permitted himself to believe that there was any such thing as ghosts or demons or anything in the least supernatural. The only supernatural aspect he permitted to enter his thoughts was the presence of the living God, the God in whom he believed even if the Almighty were incomprehensible, a God who, somehow, had concern for him while permitting or allowing or even causing the death of his beautiful wife. That was quite enough super-naturalism for him; he admitted of no other.

William continued to go to the Labrador every summer, continued to improved on his house at Kelly Cove every winter. He also continued to live there by himself, not bothering even to respond to the numerous missives from interested young women and youngish widows.

82

Tales from Harbour Divine
The Oral and Folk Story Tradition Of Western Notre Dame Bay, north east coast of Newfoundland Island

Until the summer of 1877.

From the summer of 1875, William's father and John Hewlett of Rabbits Arm had agreed that they would share their premises at Five Island Inlet, halfway down the Labrador coast, share resources, share crews, and share the returns of their fishing efforts. That summer, John Hewlett's sixteen year old daughter, Julia, had accompanied her father, as cook's helper, to the Labrador. The arrangement meant that at least one full share was saved because one cook was serving both crews. The sixteen year old girl would receive a half share.

Julia was quite attractive. She was vivacious. She was bold. She was provocative. William's heart, frozen for three years, began to thaw again.

Every Sunday, either William Ryan, the staunch Catholic, or John Hewlett, the staunch Protestant and Orangeman, would offer to take whoever was interested across the bay to Tumbler Bight where the Oxfords from Little Bay Islands regularly held divine service. Previous summers, William had spurned the opportunity to mingle with the Protestants in the singing of hymns and the direct prayers to God, bypassing the Blessed Virgin, the saints, and even Jesus himself. William was not interested in the preaching of either George Oxford or his son, Francis, although all of the other fishermen, including the Catholics, declared that to listen to the Oxfords was decidedly worthwhile.

However, William was neither blind nor lacking intelligence and couldn't help but observe two phenomena: Julia was interested in attending the religious service across the bay, and other single young men were interested in Julia. Even though he still grieved his beloved Amelia, he acknowledged that, maybe, here was a girl who might help ease his aching arms and aching heart. William acknowledged his human need of affection and companionship. In short, he wanted to capture Julia Hewlett. Thus, William II began to attend the Oxfords' divine services and contrived to sit as close as possible to the pretty Julia both on the to and return voyages and at the service itself.

Now, there were those who suggested that John Hewlett had other objectives when he allowed or encouraged his daughter to accompany him to the Labrador, that he admired the young William Ryan, his work ethic, his steadfastness, and conspired to have the girl work her magic on the young man. Whether John Hewlett had such designs or not, the maiden's magic worked.

On returning to Long Island in the autumn, William II found numerous excuses to sail the seven or eight miles in the bay to Rabbits Arm and to visit the comely Julia. By Christmas, the Hewlett family knew that the jig was up: the young people were in love. However, they waited another year to marry, when Julia was almost eighteen years old. Their wedding was celebrated at the Methodist church at Rabbits Arm on May 11, 1879. Up to this time Julia had not seen her husband's house at Kelly Cove. For the remainder of that summer, Julia remained with her mother at Rabbits Arm until the men returned from the Labrador in the autumn.

Julia loved the house, loved Kelly Cove, and looked forward to many years there with her handsome William. Julia, however, had also heard the story of the discovery of the map in the cave at the other end of the island – who didn't?. It turned out that John Hewlett was born at Western Arm and had lived there until Julia was almost thirteen years old. Julia was a fourth generation descendant of none other than Salona Simmonds. Moreover, up to the time that Julia left Western Arm, the silver tube and silver chain was, by far, the most well-known item in the village. The artifact had been passed down through the generations and, although it never came to Julia's branch of the descendants, everybody knew about the old item, everybody had seen it and handled it, and everybody knew the story, the details. Interesting objects, handed down through the generations, have the power to retain related stories.

What Julia did not know, at first, was that the Kelly Cove where she was to live with her husband was the selfsame cove associated with the map and its supposed ghosts.

But she found out that winter!

The terrible sounds of the storms were unbelievable. The horrible screechings, even during calm weather, were even worse. William was convinced that the sounds during calm weather must be from some larger bird, some sort of eagle, perhaps.

William found out that there was more to Julia than he had, heretofore, realized. She, also, had a will of steel. She, too, carried ancestral baggage that coloured her almost every breath. She was descendant from Huguenots, those French Calvinists who suffered so terribly under the French Catholics, who had their lands confiscated, who had their citizenship taken away, and who were evicted from their native land. All of the religious pride of a marginalized people rose up in Julia Hewlett like a pillar of wrought iron. Once she made a decision, she could not be moved. She was not going to be bothered by sounds on the wind. The devil take it!

Julia expected her lying-in to be mid-February. Her parents had come in mid-January to be on-hand for the event. John Hewlett was wont to read his Bible every evening while sitting by the fireplace. Sometimes he conversed with his son-in-law, sometimes about religious topics. They marveled that their ancestral stories were so similar, only their respective religions were reversed; In Ireland, the Protestants brutalized and displaced the Catholics; in France, the Catholics inflicted a veritable holocaust on the Protestants, took away their property and evicted them. It was a sobering lesson for both men.

Even though the birth was accompanied by unearthly shreakings on the wind, little Amelia first saw the light of day on February 9, 1880.

Steel-willed though she was, Julia's nerves began to go on-edge at the regular banging on the door, rapping on the windows, and raking on the clapboard.

William and Julia moved to Rabbits Arm in March so that William, with his father's approval, could go in collar and become shareman with his father-in-law, the elder William having three other sons anxious to take over when the elder of the family was ready to hand over the reigns of the schooner.

Julia was reluctant to return to Kelly Cove the following October. Her mother had noted all summer that Julia was not

86

Tales from Harbour Divine
The Oral and Folk Story Tradition Of Western Notre Dame Bay,
north east coast of Newfoundland Island

herself, not sleeping well, not able to concentrate on looking after the baby.

The couple stayed in Kelly Cove from November to February, the hauntings coming regularly, and Julia was suffering terribly under the strain. It was even beginning to affect William.

As they had done the previous year, the couple moved to the Hewlett homestead at Rabbits Arm in March. William accompanied John Hewlett to the Labrador in May, returning late in October, 1881. Julia was pregnant again.

William prepared to return to Kelly Cove. Julia didn't want to go. Only with a lot of reassurance and coaxing did she agree. In any case, they stayed with Julia's parents until almost Christmas, with William helping his father-in-law do repairs that they normally would have left for spring. It meant that William and Julia need not come to Rabbits Arm until late in April of the following spring.

Francis was born late in January, 1882. Attended as before by her mother, the birth was normal, the baby was healthy, Julia was not. The young woman began to see things, hear things, say things that made no sense. William now realized that the young woman who was his wife was losing her mind. He suspected that he might also be losing his.

Spring came early in 1882. Around mid-April, William needed to go to Lushes Bight to purchase a bit of tea and a jug of molasses. He assured Julia that he would be back by mid-afternoon. As he approached the foot bridge over the brook by which Kelly Cove Pond empties into the ocean, the bridge which he had built himself, he saw a man standing in the middle of the wooden structure. He didn't recognize the man. He was surprised. He was sure that he knew every man alive on Long Island. As he drew closer he observed that the man's clothing was that which he determined was of European design of several centuries earlier. As he was to step on the bridge, the man raised his hand:

"Thou shalt not cross!" in a deep, unearthly voice.

"What dost thou mean? I shan't cross? This is my bloomin' bridge, built with my own hands. I will cross on my own bridge!"

"Thou shalt not cross!"

"I will, too, cross. Get out of my God Damm way!"

"What does it take to make you move away?"

William stopped. "What dost mean?"

"I've taken one wife and child. Do I have to take you new wife and your new children?"

William began to sweat. Who was this man? How dare he talk about his loss and his family?

"Get off my bridge. Go to the devil!" and William proceeded to cross the bridge. As he drew near the apparition, it shrieked, "Go away! Go away! You do not belong here!"

The apparition disappeared! Just like that! One moment, it was there, plain as day; the next moment there was nothing. Nothing at all.

William continued on to Lushes Bight, convincing himself that he had imagined the whole thing, that he had had some kind of dream, that he would soon be able to look back on the incident and laugh.

As he drew near the brook on his return trip from Lushes Bight, he realized something was amiss. The bridge was gone. Completely! Not even the posts, that he had beat into the earth at least three or more feet, were remaining! What kind of ungodly force could have pulled out these pilings?

William waded the brook, getting wet to past his waist and hurried towards his home. Before he could see the house, he could hear his wife shrieking and his children wailing. Running as fast as he could, he rushed through the open door, snatched up little Amelia from the floor and tried to calm down his wife who now seemed not to recognize him. She fought him off.

He put the child in her playpen and tried to put his arms around his wife, finally catching her from behind and avoiding the knife with which she was trying to slash him, still trying to defend herself

When she realized who held her, she screamed, "Did you see them? Did you see them?"

"See who"

"Them! The ugly men! The pirates! They came in the house! They went after the babies! I fought them!"

William sadly realized that they could no longer stay at Kelly Cove, that they would have to abandon the house that he had so proudly built and with which he was so pleased.

He helped Julia get dressed. He dressed the babies. Realizing that he would not be able to get across the brook, he took them down to the landwash, launched his punt, and, just as dusk was settling, landed at Caleb Colbourne's stage head. Caleb Colbourne was married to Julia's aunt, John Hewlett's sister. Caleb was also shareman with John Hewlett, his brother-in-law.

During the next couple of days, William removed his possessions from the house at Kelly Cove and had them transported to Rabbits Arm.

William applied for and received a grant for land adjoining his father-in-law at Rabbits Arm. He built another house.

Although Julia eventually became functional and birthed six more children, she never fully recovered. She died at the village, then called Roberts Arm, on September 15, 1925 never having become a happy woman, haunted to her last moment by her experiences at Kelly Cove.

As the fishing schooner made its way from Roberts Arm out the ships' run, passing Lushes Bight and Kelly Cove on the Starboard side, on the way to Labrador, or on the port side, on its return, William would avert his eyes. He couldn't bear to look at the scene that had killed his spirit.

The old house, so proudly built, weathered the elements for almost another twenty years, eventually succumbing to the

90

Tales from Harbour Divine
*The Oral and Folk Story Tradition Of Western Notre Dame Bay,
north east coast of Newfoundland Island*

elements. Somebody, mercifully, put a match to it during the summer of 1900.

William died at Roberts Arm on September 3, 1936 never again having set foot in Kelly Cove.

Whether Kelly Cove has ghosts or demons is unknown. Whether pirate loot lies there in Kelly Cove Pond or in the adjoining bogland, or at the site of the house is a matter of conjecture. What is known is that, even to this day, after almost two hundred fifty years of myth, mystery and tragedy, nobody else has dared build a house or tried to live at Kelly Cove.

THE END

NOTES

Note 1: This story is based on information obtained from the family of William Ryan and Julia Hewlett, that is, from their children and grandchildren.

Note 2: Psychological theories exist that can explain virtually all of the experiences of William and Julia at Kelly Cove, the assumption being that Julia already had some pre-existing emotional problems and that William really didn't want to live there, that his obsession with the family motto contributed to an identity problem, and that the two people had developed an unconscious mutual conspiracy. This does not negate, however, the fact that both people were thoroughly convinced that the events actually happened. The matter of Julia's continued psychological problems would seem to support such an explanation. As of this writing, there are people still living who knew and remember both William and Julia and remember that "Aunt Julie" had something seriously wrong. She said and did strange things.

The matter of Amelia Croucher and the manner of her death, however, is much more problematic, as is the witness of the midwife and of Amelia's mother.

Note 3: The silver tube and chain have disappeared. Speculation is that one or more of the descendants of Salona Simmonds might have sold it to some collector or museum. Its estimated value, according to some assessments, is in the hundreds of thousands of dollars. It may be in some museum or in a private collection somewhere.

Acknowledgments

Appreciation is due to several of the descendants of William Ryan and Julia Hewlett for the details of this story. In particular, the contribution of their grandson, Eric Donald Ryan, of Roberts Arm, Notre Dame Bay, is hereby acknowledged.

92

Tales from Harbour Divine
*The Oral and Folk Story Tradition Of Western Notre Dame Bay,
north east coast of Newfoundland Island*

The Revival at the Methodist Church at Little Bay Islands

Francis Oxford was depressed. Labrador fishing voyages had been poor for several years. His schooner needed a major overall. His crew was disgruntled because their livin' from voyages was so inadequate. Although fair as far as the value of the voyage was concerned - that is, they knew that they had not been cheated - their income was a mere pittance. Several of them had already told Francis that they might look for a berth with some other Labrador fishing captain.

That vicious blizzard of two years ago, March 1892, had done so much damage that many wharves and stages, built with so much energy and effort, were still not fully repaired and restored. Even his schooner was not fully repaired: seaworthy, but still not fully repaired.

Francis was also despairing over his spiritual life. He was bitter with his God. He felt that God had turned His face away from him. He was angry with the Almighty Presence, or lack thereof. In fact, he hardly felt the Presence, anymore. He was not even sure that he wanted to feel the Presence, or that such a Presence even existed for him to feel.

God had taken one son from him by drowning. God had taken his adopted son through the plague that had swept across the bay over the preceding decade. Several of his daughters had been ill but, miraculously, had survived.

Francis had quarreled with his brother-in-law; he was at odds with the minister; he had been sharp with his gentle wife; he had been less than gentle with his daughters. In short, he was depressed.

The year was 1894. Francis Oxford had been lay-reader in the Unitarian-Methodist church for over 30 years, sharing the lay ministerial function with his father, Rev. George Oxford (Unitarian), until the death of that learned man in 1890. His father, George, born at Piddlehinton, Dorsetshire, had been an Oxford University trained minister who, having quarreled with his father in England, took his newly minted Master of Divinity to Newfoundland where he (1) became a Labrador fishing captain with his own schooner, and (2) joined the Methodist church, more or less, never officially because he was Unitarian to his last breath - the Wesleyan Methodist church, that is - and although disdaining, in 1843, the Methodist Conference of Newfoundland's offer of ordination and the Little Bay Islands Pastoral Charge as a full-time minister became, nevertheless, the defacto minister during the winter months when the Parson for the Nipper's Harbour Pastoral Charge managed to get to Little Bay Islands only once every five or six weeks or so .

From about 1842, when he had arrived at Little Bay Islands with his wife, the former Martha Young of Twillingate, people had flocked to the Methodist Church to hear the young George Oxford preach. The scholarly lay minister had taught his son not only sound reading and writing skills, but had also schooled him in theology and philosophy, so much so that decades before the elder George had died, barely five years ago, he considered Francis to have as much theological education as himself. Although George would continue to preach and lead worship services almost up to the year of his death, he willingly stepped aside, as often as possible, and encouraged Francis to take the pulpit. They were required in the pulpit almost three or four Sundays out of a month because, as explained, their minister had a large circuit.

Thus, on the Sundays when the minister was not there, father and son would alternate morning and evening services, one of them leading the worship, the other delivering the sermon. Sometimes, other lay members would do the scriptures and prayers. They also shared leadership of the Sunday evening after-service, the evangelical aspect of their joint ministry. Not all of the congregation would stay after the first benediction. A hymn would be sung giving the less-demonstrative members of the congregation to leave with dignity. Then, those who remained would launch into their sometimes fiery rejoicing, witnessing, and soul-winning celebration of their version of the Christian faith.

Francis Oxford was an orator par excellence! George, the father, had told Francis on numerous occasions that even though he realized it was sinful, there were times when he envied his son because of the latter's skills in elocution and his ability to explain better than the father – the Oxford trained theologian – some of the complexities of Christian theology in a manner that the least educated of the villagers could understand and appreciate.

George had brought with him from England numerous wooden boxes of theological and philosophical tomes when he abandoned the mother country, mother church, and his mother, father and siblings. He and Francis had added to the collection over the years, so that Francis now had a theological library that would be the envy of some schools of divinity. Francis had followed the practice of his father and had bookshelves installed in his captain's cabin on the schooner, had stuffed them with theology books, and went on his annual voyages to the Labrador confident that he would still be able to pursue his theological and philosophical studies.

He, Francis, also conducted regular Sunday afternoon services in whichever Labrador harbour the Oxford cousins had their rooms. His uncle, Harry (Henry) Oxford and his father had decided years ago that they would be better off sharing premises and as much as possible, otherwise, than each going it alone. This was especially true at Tumbler Tickle, where the Oxford father from 1828, then father and son, from the time that Francis was 13 years old and first accompanied his father to Labrador, held divine service. Then, when George was crippled up with arthritis and not able to continue his voyages to Labrador, Francis conducted services alone. Francis had dreamed than, in the course of time, his own, and only, son, Alvin, would follow in his footsteps.

But Alvin had drowned in Muddy Hole, there at Little Bay Islands, several springs ago when Francis had been readying for his regular voyage. Francis never recovered from the shock. Neither had his gentle wife, the former, Emma Locke, a Beothuck lady who still spoke the old language. A large congregation of fishermen regularly gathered at the Oxford rooms there on that remote coast. Fishing masters, having rooms and premises in surrounding harbours and coves would make the trip to the site of the Oxford rooms almost every Sunday morning so that their fishermen could attend divine service.

Methodists and Unitarians like themselves, Church of Englanders, and most Roman Catholics were regular in attendance. Moreover, the local people came as well: livyers, Nascopi, and Eskimos, as the Inuit were called at the time. On some Sunday afternoons, there on that desolate coast, upwards of a hundred men or more, and sometimes women and children, would be on the deck of the Martha, to participate in the singing, be blessed by the prayers, and to hear one or another of the Oxford men open Holy Writ and expound on the ways and desires of their Lord.

Francis was remembering all of this and was not remiss in expressing his gratitude that his Lord had been able to use his services for the furtherance of His kingdom. But he still felt that his Lord, the Heavenly father that he had worshiped since childhood, was far from him. Francis felt that he was wandering alone in the wilderness, alone in an unfamiliar land. From childhood, from his earliest recollections, under the gentle but persistent tutelage of his erudite father, Francis had learned the rudiments of the Christian faith, had learned to feel the presence of the Holy Spirit.

Francis never doubted that he had been surrounded by the love of God, held firmly and securely in the Everlasting Hand. Now, though, his soul had chilled within him. He was lonely for the Spirit that had seemingly abandoned him. He was no longer on his pilgrimage; he had lost his way; the fogs of doubt occluded his being; his faith had withered; his joy in the lord had dissipated. He felt alone, lonely. The God who had walked daily by his side, had gone someplace else. His brother, Jesus, was otherwise engaged.

Francis realized that part of the problem was that virtually the whole village, the harbour as well as Sully Ann's Cove where he had his house, was filled with people who were down. Virtually every family had lost children to the blight, whatever it was, some as many as four or five. The spirit seemed to have abandoned everyone, even the most devout.

Francis had attended the Board of Session of the Methodist Church in February. He was bored. Their minister, the Reverend Thomas Ballencroft, on the circuit for three years, now, had detected the dejection of Francis and had opened the meeting with a prayer in which, although not calling him by name, he called on God to bring a healing touch on those who were despairing or were in spiritual distress.

On that particular frosty night, with the wind moaning around the manse, Francis was not terribly interested in the spiritual affairs of the congregation. As the meeting droned on something was tickling the back of Francis' brain, a small voice telling him that he, himself, might be contributing to the general depression of the village because people had looked to him for so long for spiritual leadership that when he was depressed, the village, as consequence, became more depressed.

Francis had often preached on a sentiment that he shared with his father: From those whom God has richly given, much is required. Francis knew that his God had given him richly. Even though he had no diplomas, he realized that he was probably the most educated person in the whole bay, maybe on the whole north east coast of Newfoundland Island. He had been a student all his life. On voyages to the Labrador he had discussed philosophy with his father; at night, as they lay side by side in their respective humble cots at their fishing rooms, they debated points of theology. The challenged each other's logic; they challenged each other's faith.

Without knowing where the idea came from because it was out of his mouth even before he realized he was speaking, Francis Oxford said, "We need a new church!"

That was not the topic of discussion of the moment. It had not even been on the agenda. The Rev. Ballencroft was so shocked at the interruption that he almost lost his spectacles. He stared open-mouthed at his lay-reader. Jobbie Locke stared; Mrs. Alfreda Weir sat up straight; Willis Grimes blinked repeatedly; Jimmy Roberts appeared to come out of his daze - he had not been listening, much, either. Fannie Burton took out her hankie and dabbed at her eyes; Charles Mitchell, clerk of session, almost dropped his quill.

A new church?

A new Church!

The members of the session looked at each other!

How come nobody had suggested that before? The current building had been hastily built after their old church had burned about thirty years ago. The new structure had been particularly well built. Almost nobody would dispute that it had been no more than frapsed up. The roof was sagging; there was almost no way to keep it warm for services during the winter. It was not even attractive.

A new church!

They all realized that they needed a new building, raised to the glory and honour of their God.

It was some moments before the minister took control of the meeting and suggested that they all think about Brother Oxford's suggestion and that he would call a meeting of the Official Board for the very next week.

The decision was made.

A new church!

Excitement was in the air!

During the following autumn and winter, right after the schooners returned from the Labrador and the fish was shipped, the men of the congregation had spent weeks in the woods, further in the bay, slaying down saw logs which were brought home on the decks of whatever boats that could be pressed into service. Pit saws were set up, planes were sharpened. Men took turns sawing the logs, others made them smooth and even, while others cut the tongues and grooves. Other men, following drawings prepared by several of the congregation, were skillfully deploying chisels and adzes, carefully preparing sills and fitted trusts for the ceiling.

100

Tales from Harbour Divine
*The Oral and Folk Story Tradition Of Western Notre Dame Bay,
north east coast of Newfoundland Island*

On Sunday, May 12, 1895 a sod turning ceremony was held at which the whole village turned out. It was the last Sunday before the schooners were to leave for the Labrador fishery. At the end of the service, there on the hillside at the bottom of the harbour, with the wind blowing keenly off the rough ice, and seals coming up for air and barking their discant, Francis Oxford, lay reader, was called on to pray.

After the usual formalities utilized when addressing the Almighty and when seeking to enter the Divine Presence, Francis Oxford was inspired. He called on the Sovereign of the Universe to move the hearts of the people so that at the opening of the new church, there would be a revival, that the wayward people of the village would find their way to the footstool of the Lord. The conclusion of the prayer was followed by many people shouting, "Amen!" "Amen Lord I say!" (That voice over all of the others would have been that of Elija Campbell!), "Even so, Lord Jesus!" " Amen, Lord!" and such other praises and accolades that the people felt might cause their God to look down favourably upon them.

During that summer and autumn the church took shape through the painful labour of those retired fishermen crippled up with arthrits, some hardly able to stand. Sometimes, the women jloined them.

The building was weather-tight before Christmas. Clapboard and windows were installed during January, February and March. The steeple was attached in April. Meanwhile, men had been engaged in constructing pews and carving a pulpit and deacon's bench and doing up the chancel where the new organ would be installed. The new "portable" pipe organ had been ordered the autumn before from a firm at Philadelphia. It was expected to arrive sometime during the summer and would be dedicated next Autumn when all of the schooners had returned from the Labrador.

Opening ceremonies were scheduled for the first Sunday of May, the third day of the month. People had come across the bay from sister churches at Ward's Harbour, Beaumont, Lushes Bight, Jerry's Harbour, Paddock's Bight, Sunday Cove Island, Rabbits Arm, Pilley's Island, Harry's Harbour and Jackson's Cove. Several boat loads of people had even come from as far afield as Tilt Cove and La Scie and Nipper's Harbour and Western Arm on the northern side of the bay. The Conference Secretary had come all the way from St. John's to bring wishes on behalf of the Methodist Conference of Newfoundland.

The service would be held in the early afternoon so that people wishing to do so would be able to get back across the bay and to their homes before dark. As if the Almighty had caused His mighty hand to clear the way, the arctic ice was loose, winds were light and offshore. People would be able to find their way home without difficulty between the ice flows, the growlers, and the small bergs.

The new church was packed. People were excited. Several people were commenting to their neighbours that they remembered the prayer of Francis Oxford at the sod turning and wondered if anything would happen.

The church hushed. The parson, as their minister was still called, came to the pulpit and greeted the congregation and gave a special welcome to the people from other villages and an extra-special warm welcome to the Secretary of Conference. The parson asked the people to welcome the dignitary with a show of hands. If the almost deafening applause was any indication of what was in peoples' hearts, something, must surely, just have to happen!

The service opened with that wonderful hymn, *Faith of our Fathers.* Singing was robust, the organ from the old church wheezing and squeaking as Mrs. Millicent Grimes worked the pedals furiously to try to get enough air to make a bit of music. The minister prayed. Then, he explained that, in the interest of time, the usual period of witnessing would be held over to the evening service.

Then, to the everyone's evident delight, Thomas Weir, a gentle long past his middle aged known for his melodious voice, sang *The Model Church.*

The Model Church
Well, wife I found the model church
An' worshiped there today
It made me think of good ole times
Before my hair was gray
The meeting house was more finely built
Than they were, years ago
But then I found when I went in
It was not all built for show.
The sexton did not set me down
Away back by the door
He knew that I was old an' deef

And saw that I was poor
He must have been a Christian man
He led me boldily thru
The long asile of that crowded church
To find a pleasant view
I wish you'd heard the singing, wife
It had the old time ring
The preacher said, with trumpet voice
Let all the people sing
Ole Cornation, was the tune
The music up, would roll
I thought I heard the angel choir
Strike up their harps of gold.
My deepness seemed to melt away
My spirit caught the fire
I joined my feebling, trembling voice
With that melodious crowd
And same as in my youthful days
Where angels prostrate fell
Bring forth the royal diadem
And crown them Lord of all.
I tell you wife, it did me good
To sing that hymn, once more
I felt like some wrecked mariner
Who gets the glimpse of shore.
It made me want to lay aside
This weather beaten form
And anchor on that blessed shore
Forever from the storm
Twas not a flowery sermon, wife

But simple, joyful truth
It fitted 'umble men like me
It suited hopeful youth
To winning model souls to Christ
The honest preacher tried
He talked not of himself or men
But Jesus, crucyfied
Dear wife, the toil will soon be o'er
The victory soon won
The shining land is just ahead
Our home so bright an' fair
Thank God, we'll never sin again
There'll be no sorrow there
There'll be no sorrow there
There'll be no sorrow there
In the land above where all is love
There'll be no sorrow there

The congregation sat in awed silence ....

The minister, mindful of Francis Oxford's prayer at the sod turning ceremony, again stood at the pulpit and announced the next hymn, this one from the beloved *Sankey's Sacred Songs and Solos:*

Jesus, Tender Saviour
Jesus, Tender Saviour, Thou hast died for me!
Make me very thankful in my heart to Thee.
When the sad, sad story of Thy grief I read,
Make me very sorry for my sins, indeed.
Now, I know thou lovest, and dost plead for me!

Tales from Harbour Divine
The Oral and Folk Story Tradition Of Western Notre-Dame Bay,
north east coast of Newfoundland Island

105

Make me very thankful in my prayers to thee.
Soon I hope in Glory, At they side to side do stand;
Make me fit to meet thee in that Happy Land.
(H. N. Whitney)

Although the singing was enthusiastic, the Holy Spirit seemed to be elsewhere because there was no sign that It had any intention of moving very much or very far in this church, that day. The minister, who had devoutly believed that God would answer Francis Oxford's prayer, was beginning to doubt.

The Secretary of Conference came forward and passed on official greetings from the Methodist Conference and then read the scripture: Matthew, Chapter 7: 1 - 27.

Another hymn was sung and collection received. Then the Secretary of Conference came and delivered the sermon, taking as his focus texts: We love him because He first loved us, 1 John IV, 19 and Not everyone that saith unto me, "Lord, Lord," shall enter into the Kingdom of Heaven; but he that doeth the will of my father which is in heaven, Matthew 7: 21.

Upon hearing the scripture reading, and even before the Secretary of Conference began to expound upon the word, Francis Oxford felt like someone had smashed him in the side of the head with a sledge hammer. He felt convicted before the Lord! This was a chapter on which he had preached many times. This was one of the favourite chapters of his father, the revered Rev. George Oxford, now home abed, too weak to attend the service..

This was the chapter that he and his father agreed on was probably the foundation of the Christian faith. And, now, he acknowledged to himself, that for the past decade he had not been cognizant of the message, that he had been following his Lord from afar! It was all he could do to keep from weeping in self-loathing at his sinful state.

He didn't hear the message of the Secretary of Conference even though he had so looked forward to it. The later reverend gentleman was widely known as a theological scholar. Francis had hoped to hear a new argument, a new philosophical slant, a fresh perspective. He was so convicted of his own fallen state that he heard nothing.

He did, however, begin to castigate himself that maybe, over the years, without quite realizing what was happening, he had come to rely more on his own powers of logic and rationality for his spiritual sustenance than on the succor of the Spirit, that aspect of being and spirituality that lies in the realm beyond mere rationality.

The minister was feeling his own disappointment. Although the sermon of the Secretary of Conference was theological inspiring, it was not the evangelistic message that the minister had hoped for. While the congregation would, no doubt, discuss the sermon thoughtfully and comment on the intelligence of the visiting clergyman, the message, although doubtlessly stimulating to the intellect, was not insinuating itself into the hearts of the people.

The minister felt again that the Spirit of the Lord must be over on Long Island, somewhere, or away from Newfoundland altogether. One thing was certain: the Holy Spirit was not present on Little Bay Islands, even though he had done his best to invoke the Blessed Presence in his opening prayer. He, too, was dejected. The minister had been expecting something else. A miracle?

Although he had not planned to do so, before the final hymn, Parson Balloncroft announced Showers of Blessing, before which he issued the altar call.

There was less response to the altar call than if he had told them that he was going to go swatching, on the morrow, to try to get a batch of bull birds for his supper. They would certainly have been much more interested, and the bull birds would have been much closer to their hearts than was any such exalted thing as conversion or commitment or even a renewal.

There was nothing!

Several people were looking at their hands and were fidgeting as if to suggest to their parson to get on with it and let them get home to their supper of salted herrings.

The Holy Spirit was not in evidence.

Dejectedly and with resignation that he was not going to witness any outpouring of the Spirit on this otherwise wonderful day, wonderful news with which he could start off his letters to family and friends and colleagues in England, he announced the final hymn, *Guide me O Thou Great Jehovah.*

He watched the people as they stood to sing.

108

Tales from Harbour Divine
*The Oral and Folk Story Tradition Of Western Notre Dame Bay,
north east coast of Newfoundland Island*

Nothing!

The congregation launched into the hymn with gusto, but the parson knew that it was only their natural joy of singing, and had nothing whatsoever to do with either the words of the grand old hymn or of the sentiment and beliefs associated with it. He was convinced that they would have been just as happy singing one of their filthy fishing ditties, or those suggestive songs that he sometimes heard boys singing out on their floating stages. He had even heard some of the men of the congregation, good committed Christians, supposedly, singing those disgusting songs that they made up themselves.

Parson Balloncroft, late of Somerset, was angry at his flock. They were certainly not sheep, following the guidance of the Master or of he, the shepherd. Truly, they were a veritable bunch of goats, each going on in his or her independent and heedless way and manner. This was supposed to be a joyous occasion. There was supposed to be a revival, not only of their faith but of the general ethos and spirit of the village. These people needed it. They needed an infilling of the Spirit in almost as many meanings of the word as there were people in the congregation. However, obviously, it was not to be.

Anyway, he told himself, he had been in Newfoundland, in this wretched and remote outpost, far too long. Colleagues in England had written to him about the wonderful opportunities in several major up-coming industrial cities where he would be able to exhibit those intellectual skills which had won him such renown while at university.

Besides, there were anticipated openings for professors at his alma mater, Oxford University. His erstwhile scholar companions considered him a shoo-in should he deign to apply. Nobody in this isolated God forsaken backwater of creation, with the possible exception of Francis Oxford, appreciated his intellect and his theological expertise. He had stayed this final year substantially because of Francis Oxford's prayer, last May.

He had already written his letter of resignation to the Newfoundland Methodist Conference, last May, and had been about to post it, hesitating to do so only because of Francis Oxford's prayer.

Balloncroft had decided to stay. In a sense, he was putting his God to the test. He knew that it was sinful to do so, a stark defiance of the Biblical warning. He hadn't admitted to himself what he was really doing. But, today, he acknowledged to himself and to his God that he had done wrong; he had put his God to the test and God had turned His face away from him. He should have mailed his resignation as he had intended and gone home to England as he had planned.

As the last strains of that old hymn of the faith died away and as the old organ gave its last terrible screeches and wheezes, like some decrepit bagpipe gasping its final snarl, Parson Balloncroft, M.Div. (Oxon) stood to give the benediction, determining to tell The Secretary of the Newfoundland Conference of the Methodist Church, immediately after this torturous service was concluded, that he had decided to resign from the circuit, the so-called pastoral charge, and to return to England. He had no more

110

Tales from Harbour Divine
The Oral and Folk Story Tradition Of Western Notre Dame Bay,
north east coast of Newfoundland Island

pastoral left in him to give. He knew that he now doubted his God. God had not proven Himself faithful!

As the minister raised his arms to call the people to prayer, someone spoke to him. He dropped his arms and looked around. He heard the voice again: Call on Francis Oxford to give the benediction! He was astounded. Where was that voice coming from? He looked at the congregation. They were staring at him in consternation. Was their minister having an apoplexy?

He faced the congregation: Dear and faithful people, he intoned, it would be only right and proper to call on the man whose dream and inspiration this new church was. So, I am calling our dear and beloved lay-reader, Francis Oxford, to come forward to dismiss us with God's grace.

Francis Oxford, in his turn, was astounded. The minister had not told him that he was going to be called on. He had prepared nothing. He became angry. Even as he stood to his feet, he knew that he had nothing to say. The spirit of the Lord, if such existed, had abandoned him. Normally, of course, he would not have expected to be forewarned that he was to be called on to pray. In fact, normally, he enjoyed nothing more than to lead his people to the footstool of the Almighty.

Even as the fifty-six year old man stood, he seemed to feel another presence standing with him. He could feel the presence of ... of ... of whom? Was it the Holy Spirit? Was it the spirit of his friend, Jesus, whom some call the Christ? Whoever it was, whatever it was, the presence spoke to him with the voice of his father, George Oxford.

And the voice said, "Francis, my son, this is your hour. This is the moment you prayed for. Do you really believe? Even though your step has not been as faithful as it might have been for several years, Francis, even though you may have faltered, you are only human. You are not expected to bear your burdens alone, Francis. Neither are these people, your people, Francis. They need you. They have needed you. They need a revival, Francis! Give it to them."

Although he could not recollect just how he had gotten there, Francis Oxford discovered that he was already standing in his accustomed place before the altar rail, the position he always took whenever he gave the altar call, whenever he gave a benediction. Standing before the seat of contrition, the pentitant form, the communion rail, the symbol of the feet of the Almighty, the implicit door to the Throne of the Universe, he stalled.

The congregation had hushed. Even the fidgeting babies had ceased their squirming as even they seemed to feel that something had changed. Nobody said that they felt a mighty rushing wind, but they felt something.

Francis Oxford looked at the congregation, at his beloved and gentle Emma to whom he had spoken harshly, to the pew near the back row where sat his wonderful daughters with whom he had been less than gentle and several of whom had declared, at dinner, that they had no intention of attending this ritual of hypocrisy. Then, he was drawn to the right side of the church, in the middle pew, near the window, where he met the frank eyes of his brother-in-law with whom he had quarreled. Then, he looked

112

Tales from Harbour Divine
The Oral and Folk Story Tradition Of Western Notre Dame Bay,
north east coast of Newfoundland Island

at the remainder of the congregation and knew that he had let them down because of his own self-centeredness.

He raised his arms as the symbol of the Spirit of the Lord flowing out to the people. The words came barely as a whisper: "Forgive me, Lord, for I have sinned. I have been willful; I have been stubborn; I have failed thee and I have failed your flock; I have not led your lambs to the fold."

He dropped his arms. He was shaking with emotion. He fought to claim his responses. The people waited. Somebody said, "Come, Lord Jesus." He waited. Finally, he raised his arms again:

"My dear and precious people, with a humbled heart I invite you to follow me to the footstool of the Almighty. Let us enter the courts of Grace. Let us approach with humility and expectation the Throne of God, knowing that as a mother with a wayward child, we will be accepted and forgiven without reservation." He paused.

There were those who claimed that they did hear a mighty rushing wind, but it was probably simply the south westerly winds that was keeping the ice off shore, the winds that caused the spruce trees surrounding the church to sway and rustle.

People said that they had never felt anything like it before in their lives. They, they said, felt that they were in the very presence of the Holy of Holies of Creation; that they were breathing the very ether of the Lord.

Francis Oxford prayed as he had never prayed before. He poured out his longing to his Saviour God. There was no longer any reservation. He wasn't praying for himself. He was broken for his people. God was no longer a distant being but was, now, a very Presence. He could feel It all around him.

Francis stopped. Something was happening. People were fidgeting. Several were standing, praying silently along with him. Then, his brother-in-law, that stubborn man with whom he was at loggerheads, was walking up the side aisle, across the front of the church. He stopped in front of Francis, held out his hand. Francis grasped the proffered hand and began to weep. His brother-in-law released his grip and knelt at the rail. He was in the Presence of the Lord.

Then he saw Mrs. Cassie Weir move to the rail. Then, that old curmudgeon, Hezekiah Short. Then, his brother's fifteen year old lad to whom Francis had just given a berth to the Labrador.

Look!

Oh, my !

His heart could hardly contain his happiness.

He saw Thurza, beautiful beautiful Thurza, his sixteen year old daughter, the delight of his heart, rise from her seat and come up the center aisle. She kissed her father on the cheek, her tears wetting his beard, and she took her place at the rail. Other people were coming forward. Then, much to his surprise, the minister in his robes had come down from the pulpit, had grasped his hand, and then, he, too, knelt at the rail.

Suddenly, almost en mass, the congregation surged forward, those who were to give their first commitment, those seeking renewal, and even some who though it might be worth a try, even if they didn't quite believe.

There was much rejoicing! The people began to sing. Someone began to sing, "The beautiful River." The congregation joined in enthusiastically and en mass. If the new church needed a baptism as well as a dedication, it received it this Sunday afternoon with the tears of joy of the people. Even the Secretary of the Methodist Conference of Newfoundland, normally a rather reserved man, was not able to help himself. He felt like dancing! He joined in the hand clapping and the rejoicing. Parson Balloncroft didn't quite know what to do. He wanted a miracle. He was witnessing the miracle. He didn't believe the miracle. He abandoned himself to the rejoicing. Now was not the time for intellectualizing.

Francis Oxford, having once again found the core of his faith, was surrounded by his gentle Martha and his girls. There would be no talk of hypocrisy around their family table for a long long time. Even, years later, when the daughters had left home and had gone to Canada and the United States, they would write letters home to Thirza or Leah, the two sisters who stayed in Newfoundland, and say that what they remembered most about their tender years was the wonderful revival and how much the old hymn still meant to them:

Tales from Harbour Divine
*The Oral and Folk Story Tradition Of Western Notre Dame Bay,
north east coast of Newfoundland Island*

115

Beautiful River

Shall we gather at the river
Where bright angel feet have trod;
With its crystal tide forever
Flowing by the throne of God?
CHORUS: Yes, we'll gather at the river,
The beautiful, the beautiful river --
Gather with the saints at the river
That flows by the throne of God.

On the margin of the river,
Washing up its silver spray,
We will walk and worship ever,
All the happy, golden day. Cho.

On the bosom of the river,
Where the Saviour-king we own,
We shall meet, and sorrow never
'Neath the glory of the throne. Cho.

Ere we reach the shining river,
Lay we every burden down;
Grace our spirits will deliver,
And provide a robe and crown. Cho.

At the smiling of the river,
Rippling with the Saviour's face,
Saints, whom death will never sever,
Lift their songs of saving grace. Cho.

Soon we'll reach the shining river,
Soon our pilgrimage will cease,
Soon our happy hearts will quiver
With the melody of peace. Cho.
(Robert Wadsworth Lowry: 1826 - 1899)

When the final tally was in, it was determined that there were thirty seven new converts, not counting the numerous renewals: twelve men, fourteen married women, and eleven young people who had sought and found the grace of forgiveness at the footstool of their Lord..

The revival was talked about for years.

The End

Note: Francis Tizzard Oxford served his congregation for another fourteen years, going to his eternal rest in 1910, at age 70. His wife, the former Emma Locke, remarried to George Parsons of Lushes Bight. After the latter's death, Emma moved to Roberts Arm to live with daughter Thirza and family. Emma died in 1932.

Thirza loved to tell this story, and tell it she did, dozens and dozens of times, almost always leaving her audience with gentle tears

The Nugget of Gold

Harbour Divine is a small fishing village in Notre Dame Bay whose origins go back to at least the mid-1700s of the current historical cycle. Until about 1875, it remained the home of a dozen or so families devoted to the fishery and subsistence farming. After the mines closed at Pilley's Island, Little Bay and Tilt Cove, all in the late 1800s, several families moved to Harbour Divine rather than to go off to Glace Bay, or elsewhere, preferring to stay in Newfoundland.

The Tilson family was one such, the head of which, Martin Tilson, was a middle-aged mining engineer who had received serious injuries in a mine explosion and could no longer work in his old capacity. The learned man managed to look after his family with a little fishing and some farming, covering his basic financial needs with a little money from some unknown source and about which there was much speculation. In any case, he was not in hoc to the local merchant.

Samuel Tilson, Martin's 18 year old son, already a full Labrador shareman with Elijah Parsons out of Lushes Bight, had been squiring Sadie Matchford for more than a year. Sadie had already told her mother that she expected that Samuel would soon be asking her to marry him and that she was happily anticipating the auspicious day.

Sadie, pretty, intelligent - she knew how to read! - had one characteristic which the whole community knew about and

118

Tales from Harbour Divine
*The Oral and Folk Story Tradition Of Western Notre Dame Bay,
north east coast of Newfoundland Island*

sometimes scorned: she was a joker. Some people expressed the sentiment that they never knew when to take her seriously. Sadie enjoyed confounding people, waiting a few days, then clearing up any misunderstandings. People used to shake their heads whenever they spoke of the girl, saying such things as, "If tis not lies she tells, tis awful close. She's goin ta get caught in 'er own web one a dees days, you mark me words!"

Samuel arrived back from the Labrador in early October, 1885, and spent virtually every evening, thereafter, with Sadie, sometime staying until the wee hours. In fact, sometimes he stayed virtually the whole night. Crass Rowsell said, "I zeed dat boy goin' 'ome wen I was already out on me stage getting ready ta go doun da run ta get a bit a winter feesh."

Sure enough, on Sunday evening - October 25, two weeks shy of Samuel's nineteenth birthday - the young couple were walking home together from the Methodist service, gently poking fun at Carn Croucher's prayer and Mrs. Fanny Pilson's testimony in the afterservice. As they passed the one-room schoolhouse, Samuel directed Sadie towards the building and had her sit on the steps. As the full autumn moon rode high in the crisp clear sky, it was there that he made his declaration and popped the question: "Sadie, I love you. Will you marry me?"

Oh, how Sadie wanted to cry out, "Yes! Yes! Just name the date!"

But, she didn't.

Sadie couldn't resist making a joke. "Wellllll, she said, I don't know. I really don't think so. You'll never be anything but a fisherman. We knows that. I want to be rich. It's not like you could pick up a lump of gold whenever we wanted a little bit of money."

Samuel said nothing. He helped her to her feet and walked her to her gate in silence. He declined the invitation to "come in for a cup of tea," bussed her on the cheek and not on the proffered lips, turned his back to her without saying anything, and walked away.

Sadie was a little concerned, but more amused than anything. She determined that she would clear up the little joke when she saw Samuel on Monday evening. It was a shame that he had gone home early, though, with the moon high in the sky and shining brightly in through her bedroom window. They wouldn't even need a candle.

Much to Sadie's surprise, Samuel didn't come to visit on Monday evening. She was somewhat concerned but knew, for sure, that he would come tomorrow. Samuel didn't come on Tuesday evening, either. So, on Wednesday morning, very early, as soon as her younger siblings had gone to school, Sadie pushed herself across the harbour in her father's sixteen foot tarred punt glancing, occasionally, at the steel grey sky. She tied up at Martin Tilson's stagehead and walked up the wharf to the house. She entered the house without knocking, as was the custom, finding Mamie Tilson at the kitchen table kneeding a batch of bread.

Mamie looked up. "Oh, tis you. I didn't expect to see you again. What do ya want?"

"I wants ta see Samuel. Where is he?"

120

Tales from Harbour Divine
The Oral and Folk Story Tradition Of Western Notre Dame Bay,
north east coast of Newfoundland Island

"You wants ta see Samuel? He come ome Sunday night and tole us wat appened, and now you wants ta see im???" Mamie was clearly upset.

"Where is he?"

"He left Monday morning. We aven't eard from'n sunce. We don't know wat ee's gone and dun. We'm afeard dat ee's gone and dun away wit hees-self. And tis your fault." Mamie wiped her reddened eyes with her apron. Clearly, she had done a lot of weeping.

"But, I wus jokin! Ee knowed I wus jokin!" and Sadie began to cry.

"Den, twus a poor joke, Sadie, a poor joke."

As Sadie left the house and walked down the wharf, tears were falling faster than the first blossoms of winter snow that had just begun to settle from the pregnant clouds.

Time passed, days into weeks into months. Nobody heard anything from Samuel. Martin and Mamie declined the Methodist minister's offer to conduct a memorial service for Samuel whom everybody had now given up for dead. Several people, however, such as that opinionated loud-mouth, old lantern jaws himself, Garfield Puddleton, who happened to be Clerk of Session, declared to whoever would listen that, " a twould be a sin again da Lard to ave a memorial service fer da loikes a Sam Tilsen, if ee went and maed away with is-selv." Many others agreed.

At the same time, other people, devoid of sympathy for the pathetic girl, and clearly forgetting Corinthians 13, on which the

Methodist minister had preached no later than the Sunday after Samuel's disappearance, opined, "Serves her proper. Maybe, now, she'll give up dat infernal devilish ways a ern, always goin on wit stuff, almost as bad as blagard. Wat's da diference, anyhow, atween dat an enny odder sin?" No doubt, they would regret their lack of charity in the course of time and seek divine forgiveness for the momentary lapse in their practice of Christian virtues.

In the meantime, Sadie discovered that she was going to have a baby. As soon as the news got around the harbour, people tittered and some, behind their hand, said, "Well, she's goin ta git eer lump a gold, enyhow."

Virtue Samuella Matchford entered the world on July 15, a beautiful plump little girl with deep brown eyes and, eventually, thick auburn hair - the spittin image, some said, of the disappeared Samuel. Virtue was baptized In the Methodist church three weeks afterward, her grandfather, Martin Tilson standing in for the lost Samuel.

Time passed. Eventually, Sadie began to "see" Clarence Puddleton and they were married in May, 1897. Sadie gave birth to a boy the following August. She brought another baby boy into the world in September, 1888.

It was learned - some time later when the post master broke his vow of confidentially - that the Tilsons received a letter from the United States on the first trip northward of the Prospero in late May, 1889. The people of the village were astounded to watch Martin and Mamie Tilson, along with their four children, push across the harbour and board the Prospero, two weeks later, as the government mail steamer was working its way south.

122

Tales from Harbour Divine
*The Oral and Folk Story Tradition Of Western Notre Dame Bay,
north east coast of Newfoundland Island*

Nobody had any forewarning, not even Mamie's sister who was married in the vlllage. People later realized that the merchant, Chas Dolder, must have known because he had already purchased the Tilson property.

A month later, on the next northward voyage of the Prospero, Sadie received a small package, addressed in her maiden name. The package contained a letter and a gold nugget on a golden chain. The letter, from Samuel, with an address in Montana, read:

Dearest Sadie,

You will please forgive me for not writing before. But, before, I had nothing to offer you. Now, however, I do. After leaving home, I rowed to Pilley's Island and waited for the Prospero. I worked my way to St. John's, then to Halifax, next to Boston, and then to New York City. There I heard of the gold rush in the Yukon. I took a ship right around South America up to California and from there to Skagaway, Alaska. Because I could read and write, I didn't have to actually go to the gold fields, but began to make enormous money in other capacities, including as a gold trader. I won't give you the details, but I am now more wealthy than I could ever have though possible. I will have no difficulty giving you a nugget of gold whenever you want.

I am offering to return to Harbour Divine so that we can marry and then return to the United States. Otherwise, I can send you the money so that you can come to me. I have no intention of returning permanently to Newfoundland.

The letter contained other details which is of no interest, here, other than Samuel telling her that he had sent his parents money for them to leave Newfoundland to come to Montana and that he anticipated seeing them in the near future.

Wisely, Sadie put the gold nugget away, saying that it belonged to Virtue.

In July, 1911, the then fifteen year old Virtue announced to her mother that she wanted the gold nugget and chain because she was going to sell it and go to the United States to look for her father. She was surprised that Chas Dolder not only wouldn't purchase the valuable necklace, but gave her some money that he said had been left to her by her grandfather, Martin Tilson. He explained that it as the proceeds from the sale of the Tilson propery.

Virtue left on the *Prospero* last week of August, 1911.

Before Christmas, Sadie received a letter from Virtue, with an address in Arizona. The girl said that she had found her father and grandparents. She had been acknowledged and welcomed. She knew that she would never be in want for money again.

Virtue never returned to Newfoundland.

Sadie died in the early 1950s and is buried in the old Methodist cemetery at Harbour Divine.

Sadie never did stop her "joking."

The End

124

Tales from Harbour Divine
*The Oral and Folk Story Tradition Of Western Notre Dame Bay,
north east coast of Newfoundland Island*

Acknowledgments:

This story is an adaptation of a tale that I heard Grandfather Abner Anthony, of Roberts Arm, Notre Dame Bay, relate to visitors on many occasions. Some of these visitors – such as Harry Anthony of Pilley's Island - knew the story as well as Abner did. My mother, Stella Ryan, also recalls hearing the story from another source.

The Seventh Daughter

Early in November, 1838, a few weeks after Michael Locke returned from the Labrador fishery, he took to wife, at the Methodist Church at Little Bay Islands, Maisie.

Maisie had no last name. In fact, Maisie was the name that Michael had given her, having had her baptised by the Methodist parson just the day before the wedding. Maisie did have another, but it was some savage name that he couldn't pronounce and did not know the meaning of, in any case. As it was, he was barely able to converse with his wife because she spoke almost no English and he the mere rudiments of her mother tongue, whatever it was. The saving grace was that his mother was able to converse with her, happily, in fact. It was also a relief to Maisie who had little if any comprehension at all of any of the ritual that she was experiencing.

Maisie understood ritual, of course. Her people had numerous rituals. She simply didn't understand the details of these particular rituals. Michael's mother explained the intent and importance of the rituals to her future daughter in law. Maisie understood the purpose of the ritual and was, of course, acquiescent.

As the Methodist parson dipped his finger in the chalice and made the sign of the cross on the girl's forehead, and told her that her name was now Maisie, she understood. It was not at all unusual for her own people to change a person's name, particularly if one was being adopted into the community, the tribe. As Michael's mother instructed her, she bowed at the appropriate places and she repeated the commitment of adult baptism as required by the protocols of the Methodist Conference of Newfoundland. She repeating after Michael's mother, as the older lady translated, about how she believed in a God of which she never heard before. She knew about a god, of course, just not this particular one.

Maisie didn't particularly like her new name but guessed it was probably as good as any other of the names that these white folk gave to each other. Michael's mother had already told her that her own White folk name was Patience which meant very powerful medicine to the White folk. She was told that her own name, Maisie, meant faithful one, about which Maisie was pleased. She knew that her new name described at least some of what she knew about herself.

Maisie also understood the nature and purpose of the marriage ritual, having observed and witnessed a number of marriages among the young people of her tribe. She had also witnessed marriages of older folk when one or another of a couple had been widowed. As at her baptism, she repeated the vows as Patience translated for her. In fact, although the words were different and although these folk were using another name for the Almighty one, she thought that there was very little about the ritual, other than language itself, that she would not have anticipated. She was committing herself to love and care for the handsome young man who was to become her husband.

This was all fine with her but, in her opinion, totally unnecessary. She had already told him that she loved him and would care for him as, she supposed - hoped, anyhow - that he would love and care for her. But, then, they couldn't converse with each other very well in language, yet. Although Michael did know some of her language, having learned it from his mother, she knew absolutely no English.

Maisie was awkward about making her sign in the book. Maisie had a sign but wondered if that was what she should use. She was about to make her own sign - 风花 , which meant Wind Flower - when Patience stopped her by putting her hand over the girl's. Maisie had almost committed a mistake, a mistake of honour, a mistake that would have been an insult to her new people. Patience then explained that the sign that she was to make on the book was the sign representing the god of these people, an X. Maisie trembled as she marked on the White folk's paper the sign of their god. That was strange! Then her husband made his sign, but Maisie was quick to observe that Michael did not use the sign of the White folk's god, but a veritable snow storm of inexplicable symbols joined together in a long line. She reminded herself that, one day, she would ask her husband why she had to use the sign of their god, while he used some other symbol or symbols.

She had already know, before she had come south on the big boat, that Michael's mother was her father's sister. She had also just discovered that Aunt Patience had not yet been given her adult name before she had left her tribe. She, also, had not received her adult name. But, then, adult names were conferred by the husband upon marriage. Thus, both she and Aunt Patience had received adult names from the white folk. She was curious and amused.

128

Tales from Harbour Divine
The Oral and Folk Story Tradition Of Western Notre Dame Bay,
north east coast of Newfoundland Island

Maisie was grateful that Aunt Patience could converse easily with her and, she discovered, at least six or seven other women of the village spoke her mother language and, thus, were able to help her settle into her new village with her new tribe and a new way of life. She was excited. She would, henceforth, live in a White folk's house and not wander in the Labrador wilderness. Moreover, she learned from Aunt Patience that, before the end of the winter, she would have her very own house. She could hardly believe it.

Maisie did receive her very own house before winter's end, and she was happy that the Almighty One had given her such a handsome, skilled, and tractable husband. Moreover, he was kind and gentle. It was almost too much to have asked for and certainly more than she had expected. She was happy. Moreover, she was more than happy that she was growing a baby, but sad that he husband was preparing to leave her for all of the spring and summer and much of the autumn: from snow to snow, she was told, fully half of the year. Michael was now able to converse with her sufficiently to explain that he had not had a summer at home, at Little Bay Islands, since his fourteenth year and that if all went well, he might not have another summer at home until he was a very old man, too old to go to the Labrador as a fisherman. The older fishermen were wont to say, "I 'aven't seed the green since I wus thirteen year old," because it was still winter when they left home to go to Labrador, and already winter when they returned .... although they may have been utilizing a little hyperbole because, some years, the snow had gone several weeks before they left home, and in fact, winter had not commenced until after several weeks after they had returned in the autumn.

The Oral and Folk Story Tradition Of Western Notre Dame Bay, north east coast of Newfoundland Island

But, their point was understood.

Consequently, unlike with the tribe of her girlhood, her present tribe required the women to look after home and family for half a year at a time. Besides that, she was expected to learn how to plant vegetables and to look after them and harvest them so that they would have sufficient food for the winter. She now understood that the two tribes - the tribe of her childhood and that of her husband - were alike in many respects, the primary one being that starvation was an evil for both peoples and that only hard work would keep that demon from their door.

Michael was not quite sure just how old his young wife was; neither did she. Her people, the wanders of the Labrador forests, didn't consider it terribly important to keep track of those sorts of things. Moreover, they seemed not to need more than the digits of one hand to do their necessary counting. More than that was simply, many. Only rarely did they need to resort to the digits of a second hand in order to transact the business of their daily tasks.

The most important counting necessity was keeping track of the years between their meetings with other tribal groups in order to exchange stories, cultural lore, hunting and other important information, but mostly to exchange women, girls, actually, who would be taken to wife by the young men of the receiving tribe. Men never ever left their home tribe.

Maisie's tribe had been meeting every four years with tribes from across the great land, those of her people who spent a great deal of time on the shores of the ocean where the sun set while her own tribe spent much of their time on the shores of the ocean where the sun rose. There didn't seem to be much other difference in the nature of life between the two groups of tribes – they hunted the same types of animals and fish, made clothing and shelters in the same manner, had the same values and expectations of individuals and groups, had the same rituals. There were some minor language differences, some minor ritual differences, and that was about it. After all, they were the same people.

Thus every four or five years, as agreed upon, Maisie's tribe made their way west right after the summer fishing season on the Labrador coast, headed for the appointed meeting place . They never worried about getting lost. They knew that should they stray, the little men, the benign hairy denizens of the Labrador wilderness, would leave signs that would enable the travelers to easily find their way. They might not see these little men, but the people of the wilderness knew that they were there, knew that they wanted to help, and knew that these strange beings could be relied on should their tribe need assistance. These little people might never reveal themselves visually, but the people were always aware of their presence. It was an article of faith with them, an aspect of their spirituality as old as the ages.

Michael returned to Little Bay Islands in October, 1841, fresh from his summer's fishing on the Labrador, to be joyously reunited with his wife and to be introduced to his infant son.

When Michael returned from the Labrador in Autumn, 1842, he met his second son, only to have to bury him a few weeks later. When he arrived home in late October 1844 he was devastated.

His wife was inconsolable. Their four year old son had died with a fever in July, and an infant son, born in August, had died within a few days of birth.

In the spring of 1845, now-childless, and consequently disconsolate, Maisie refused to stay at Little Bay Islands for the summer and insisted on accompanying her husband north with the schooner. She spent the whole of the summer with her people, not having seen any of them for over five years. She was, however, happy to return to Little Bay Islands in the autumn. Although she now realized that the so-called White folk had many difficulties in maintaining an adequate level of sustenance, clothing and shelter, their problems almost paled into insignificance in comparison with the difficulties of her own people fated to trek the wilds of the Labrador wilderness, totally dependant on the vagaries of weather and wildlife, having to live by one's wits almost moment by moment. She appreciated how exhausting it was for her forest dwelling people.

When Michael returned from the Labrador in early November, 1846, his wife had given birth to another healthy boy. He was to thrive and lived to be an old man, finally expiring in 1926.

The people of Little Bay Islands were now interested in how many sons the couple had had: four in succession, even if only one had, thus far, survived.

Maisie presented her husband with another son in November, 1848 and a sixth son in December, 1850.

By this time, people in the surrounding villages were becoming interested in the growing family. They wondered if there might be another son, a seventh son. A seventh son of a seventh son would bring good luck to everybody. Michael was a seventh son.

The myth and tradition of the special powers and qualities of a seventh son of a seventh son derive from stories and legends with their origins in the dim mists of history, in cultural traditions that predate Christianity, and in virtually all European cultures. Moreover, Holy Writ itself contains numerous references to the phenomena, so much so that devout people saw no inconsistency between their mythology and their religion. Seven was a magic number, even in Holy Writ.

Even seventh sons were deemed to be lucky, to be healers, to have a special relationship with the forces of the cosmos, to be looked on favourably by the gods, all of the gods. The powers of a seventh son of a seventh son were many times stronger. There are even legends that the seventh son of a seventh son is, in fact, not really of human origin at all, that his mother is the most powerful goddess in the spiritual realm and his father the most powerful god. The names of the gods, of course, depend on the culture. The abodes of the gods likewise have their sources in the cultural mythology of various peoples, from *Valhalla* in the mythology of the Norse, to the *Elysian Fields* in the traditions of the ancient Greeks, the *Western Isles* in certain Celtic and Druidic traditions, and numerous other concepts of after-life paradisaical abodes in between. Only the names were different. They all seem to be more or less the same heavenly sanctuary, more or less, with the same gods and goddesses, more or less, the unique characteristics varying with the values and beliefs of the particular people.

In short, the seventh son of the seventh son was special. The people of western Notre Dame Bay, from the Catholics of Fortune Harbour, the Church of Englanders of Leading Tickles, and the Methodists of Sunday Cove Islands, to the Catholics of Harbour Round, the Church of Englanders of Western Arm, and the Methodists of Snooks Arm and everybody else in between, were keeping the couple in their prayers. A seventh son of a seventh son! What a happy event that would be!

Whenever people from one village met people from another, and especially from Little Bay islands, the question was always, "Has the seventh son of the seventh son been born yet?"

Before Michael left for the Labrador in mid-May, 1852, Maisie was well along in her seventh pregnancy. The news had gone around the bay.

Except .... Maisie did not share in the anticipated joy of her new people. Even a seventh son, let alone a seventh son of a seventh son, in the culture of her aboriginal people meant danger.

A seventh son was evil. She shared her fears with Patience who assured her that she had also believed the same thing but she had changed her mind. She had been reassured that the White peoples had for thousands of generations cherished seventh sons and seventh sons of seventh sons, in particular, had rejoiced at their births, and held them in high esteem.

134

Tales from Harbour Divine
The Oral and Folk Story Tradition Of Western Notre Dame Bay, north east coast of Newfoundland Island

Maisie, although not quite convinced, was mollified. She was happy that she would not have to smother her seventh son at birth if, indeed, her seventh child turned out to be a boy. Seventh sons in her tribe were not permitted to live. Tribal traditions and myths and legends ascribed evil to seventh sons. Their ancestral experiences had been traumatic, indeed; they were not prepared to permit another to live.

The boy was born a week before Michael returned from the Labrador. The village was ecstatic! The Methodist church was filled to capacity on the Sunday morning, three weeks later, when Michael and Maisie's infant son was presented to their Lord, given the name Charles and was received into the Christian Church.

Charles Locke, like his four other surviving brothers, was a healthy boy and grew in favour with the gods and with men. He was gentle if robust, kind if sometimes brash and needing reining in by one or other of his parents, intelligent if sometimes needing chiding at the village school, brave even if sometimes foolhardy, sometimes falling in the water when he was copying on the batticaters and harbour ice while trying to outdo his companions with their feats of jumping from ice pan to ice pan.

The boy had experienced hardly a single sick day in his life. His companions thought it fun to put an earthworm in Charles' palm and watch it curl up, die, split open, and its oil gather in a little pool, one of the sure signs of the latent power of a seventh son of a seventh son.

Tales from Harbour Divine
*The Oral and Folk Story Tradition Of Western Notre Dame Bay,
north east coast of Newfoundland Island*

135

People with tooth ache sought out Charles. His palm on the side of the face or his finger on the offending tooth would ease the pain if not make it go away completely; his touch would cause a wound to cease bleeding or, at least, reduce the flow to manageable proportions; his palm on the belly of a pregnant woman would almost surely lead to an easy birth - easier, anyway, the women were convinced.

Charles was cherished in the village. Even grizzled old fishing masters were pleased to have Charles visit their vessels because his presence, even only on the deck, even only for a brief moment, would make their boats lucky and would almost surely lead to a better fishing season. If one or another of these boats didn't have a particularly good fishing season, then it was due to other adverse causes; if one or another of these fishing vessels didn't make it home but sunk in a storm on the way down the coast, then the fault did not lie with Charles. Nobody considered Charles a god; nobody thought that he was magic; but everybody felt that it was better to have his touch and his blessing and his presence than not to have it.

Charles grew. He was a healthy specimen of Newfoundland manhood, darker than his European ancestors, lighter than his Aboriginal ones, dark hair, dark eyes. Under summer's son, he burned almost black, maybe blacker than his brothers and cousins and others of his companions with similar ancestry, which was virtually all of them.

By the time Charles was thirteen years old he was already an accomplished inshore fisherman, able to use the razor-sharp fisherman's knife to gut and de-head a codfish and remove its sound-bone in four quick flashes. He became so skilful that he could do it without looking, much like the other fishermen. If one had to watch the knife all of the time, then one would not be able to clean codfish very quickly. Oh, he got a few nicks and scratches from the knife, but none very serious.

In the spring of his fourteenth year, Charles accompanied his father to the Labrador fishery. During the summer of that year he saw a girl! A beautiful girl! A girl from the forests of the Labrador wildness; a girl with beautiful clothing, finely tanned leathers, skillfully and carefully fabricated, tastefully decorated with a variety of geometric designs. He was smitten. He met her because she was his cousin, the daughter of his mother's brother.

Three years later, when Charles was almost seventeen years old, he determined that he would make his pitch for Little Sparrow whom he judged to be at least fourteen years old, now, and thus old enough to become his wife. She had already developed all of the characteristics of a woman. Many girls had already been taken to wife when much younger and much less physically mature than this beautiful dark skinned girl of the wilderness.

Although he acknowledged to himself that she might still be a little young to take as wife, he was determined to have her before some other young man did. His father approached the girl's father on Charles' behalf. This was Michael's own brother-in-law whom he knew reasonably well and visited every summer. He made young Charles' intention known but came away disappointed. Charles' hopes were shattered. There was a problem.

Tales from Harbour Divine
The Oral and Folk Story Tradition Of Western Notre Dame Bay,
north east coast of Newfoundland Island

137

The girl was a seventh daughter! Moreover, the girl was the seventh daughter of a seventh daughter! The girl's mother, from a tribe who lived by a large river that ran into the western sea, had been a joyful acquisition by her receiving tribe and had been released but reluctantly by her home tribe. The matriarchs of her home tribe, wanting desperately to keep her but, finding no suitable mate, apparently had no option but release her. The reasoning was complex and known only unto the matriarchs. Their decision was final. They couldn't keep the girl.

The daughter was lovely, the daughter was gentle, and she was lucky. Not only had the mother brought luck to the tribe, but she had produced a seventh daughter. How lucky could they be? For not a single winter since the birth of the seventh daughter had the tribe gone hungry. They had no difficulty finding game; they had caught a plentiful supply of their red fleshed fish; they had garnered lots of furs, sufficient for their own use and for trade with the white merchants. There had not been a single accidental death in the tribe in the past thirteen years; fewer difficult pregnancies; not a single mother had died giving birth since the seventh daughter of a seventh daughter had been born to the tribe.

Just how the mythology of the seventh daughter grew up within the Aboriginal tribes of Labrador seems to be as lost in the mists of their own past as are the legends of the seventh son within European culture. Speculation suggests that it may have been learned from European traders with whom these people of the woods had contact, now, for almost two hundred years. But, it may have grown up with a life of its own, just as similar

138

Tales from Harbour Divine
The Oral and Folk Story Tradition Of Western Notre Dame Bay,
north east coast of Newfoundland Island

mythology grew in European cultures. Whether the legends grew within each culture independently because of real phenomena associated with seventh sons of seventh sons, or whether the legends stemmed from a common source may never be known for certain.

What is known, however, although seemingly lesser known is that mythology associated with seventh daughters, and with seventh daughters of seventh daughters, is also well established within European cultures, particularly those having Celtic and Druidic mythology. Seventh daughters were believed to be blessed by the Goddess and were especially sought as midwives and as attendants at bedside when women were ill. They also had special healing powers. If the powers of seventh daughters and of seventh daughters of seventh daughters was less than that of seventh sons of seventh sons, it was by a mere insignificant amount. Villages with seventh daughters of seventh daughters were about as well pleased as those with seventh sons of seventh sons.

Why does the significant of seventh daughter of the seventh daughter not have a place in the mythology of the outports of western Notre Dame Bay? Nobody seems to know. It has been suggested that one of the reasons may be that the phenomenon is so rare. Nobody can remember any family having a seventh daughter in succession and even when a seventh child is a daughter, there seems to be no particular notice of the event. It may be that the powers of such a girl has lain dormant or latent or simply unrecognized because it was not anticipated.

In contrast, when the seventh child is a son, even with intervening daughters, he is still considered to have special powers, even if they may be a somewhat lesser than a fully-fledged seventh son in an unbroken succession of sons. In any case, the seventh son of a seventh son, even if is merely the seventh child of a seventh child, the boy is deemed still to have special powers.

Charles was determined to claim "Little Sparrow" to be his wife. He could not put her out of his mind. All during the summer, all during the succeeding winter at Little Bay Islands, Little Sparrow filled his every dream and almost his every waking moment. His mother had compassion for her son and was concerned with his obsession and his sense of loss. They conversed, in the language of her people. She had spoken the Labrador Cree language with her sons right from their birth. If they were not quite fluent, they spoke the language sufficiently to converse in the language at will.

It may have been his facility with the language that endeared him to Little Sparrow. She was willing even if the elders, the matriarchs, were not. Little Sparrow had already given Charles her promise; she had nothing else to give, at this stage, or almost nothing. There was still one arrow in her quiver, the one weapon of last resort that resides in every woman's arsenal, to be used or with-held at her will. Little Sparrow had already determined that she would with-hold the pleasure of her body from every other suitor. She wanted to go live with Charles and become the young man's wife. She would, however, prefer to do it with the matriarchs' blessing rather than without it. She was as determined as Charles and she had told him so.

140

Tales from Harbour Divine
The Oral and Folk Story Tradition Of Western Notre Dame Bay,
north east coast of Newfoundland Island

Charles mother told her son what he should do. She knew her people. She had an idea of what might turn the tide in the lad's favour.

On his return to the Labrador coast in May of his eighteenth year, 1870, he could hardly contain his eagerness. They landed at Silver Fox Tickle last Friday of May, the usual place where they met the Labrador natives, primarily for socialization and to renew friendships. The Newfoundland relatives always had gifts for their Labrador wilderness relatives and in-laws: tobacco, dried beans, dried peas, dried apricots, dried apple, dried prunes, a loaf of sugar. The gift didn't amount to much, cost wise, but they were eagerly awaited and gratefully appreciated by the denizens of the Labrador wilds.

This summer there was a problem. Only the men and older boys were at the gathering place. The women, girls, and younger children were living at a secluded location further inland. Charles knew that the game was up. The tribe was not going to release Little Sparrow.

Michael left the schooner and rowed down the shore to the Aboriginal encampment. He was cordially welcomed by his brother-in-law, White Wolf, the girl's father. The proud Indian man was embarrassed. He respected Michael, the man he thought of as his Newfoundland cousin, a respect that was always reciprocated, and he obviously wished to stay in his cousin's good graces. However, the tall dignified gentleman of the forest had been over-ruled by the women. Little Sparrow could not be released. He revealed to Michael that the matriarchs had found a suitable mate for Little Sparrow but that their princess was resisting, having already threatened to do her self harm.

The tribe was in a quandary. These proud people could not imagine a seventh daughter doing herself harm. What dreadful horrors would descend on the tribe should that happen?

But the matriarchs were adamant: they couldn't afford to lose the luck embodied in the girl.

Charles decided to take matters into his own hands. Following his mother's advice, he approached his uncle, White Wolf. He explained to his uncle that he was a seventh son of a seventh son. His uncle didn't believe him, didn't believe that his brother-in-law, whom he had known for over thirty years, could possibly be a seventh son.

Charles kicked over a stump, then a rock, and found what he was seeking - a humble earthworm. The lad placed the worm in his palm and his astonished uncle watched, first with curiosity, then in fascination, and finally in horror, as the worm curled up, died, split open and wasted its bodily oils in a small pool in the boy's hand. The boy turned around and, without saying anything else, walked back to the beach, pushed off his punt and went aboard the schooner.

Within minutes a half dozen men of his Uncle's tribe gathered on the beach demanding to speak with Michael. Michael went ashore and confirmed that, indeed, not only was he, himself, a seventh son, but that Charles, also, was a seventh son - the seventh son of a seventh son. Michael did not explain that such a son was considered sacred among the White folk

142

Tales from Harbour Divine
*The Oral and Folk Story Tradition Of Western Notre Dame Bay,
north east coast of Newfoundland Island*

and he did nothing to alleviate the fear now patently obvious among the aboriginal men. His wife had explained the aboriginal understanding of a seventh son, how they feared such a person, and with what dispatch such a male died before it could draw it's first breath or make it's first cry. Michael would use the knowledge to his son's advantage.

Now fearful, backing away from Michael as if expecting him to call fire from the heavenly places down upon them and their kin, the Aboriginal men disappeared into the thicket of spruce trees but reappeared further down the beach where their canoes were hauled up on the shingle. Leaving only a skeleton crew to look after their nets, they hasten down the coast, apparently heedless of the dangerous waves that had developed consequent to the easterly winds that had been freshening all morning.

Next morning, which happened to be Sunday, about a dozen aboriginal canoes had gathered about a quarter mile down the beach. One canoe detached itself from the group and approached the schooner. White Wolf and another man were paddling, the maiden sitting in the midsection. He hailed Michael, but refused to come aboard the schooner to share breakfast as, previously, he was happy to do.

The canoe drew alongside the schooner where White Wolf held the rope ladder while the girl ambled across the canoe and climbed to the deck, assisted by willing hands of the crew. White Wolf turned his face away from his daughter and refused to watch her as she left her old world and embraced, and was embraced by, her new.

Again, Michael tried to persuade White Wolf to come aboard, but he refused. Without further ado, the two dark men, with as much dignity as they could muster, pushed away from the schooner and paddled back toward their tribal group. Before doing so, however, White Wolf performed a ritual that none of the schooner's fishing crew had witnessed before. He reached into the ocean, splashed handfuls of water around the fragile craft he was piloting, and then wiped his face and arms with his hands.

Little Sparrow, in obvious horror, fell to the deck of the schooner. Her father had disowned her, declared her dead, and had erased her from his own and his tribe's memory. She would never again be welcomed within the boson of the tribe. She no longer existed.

Michael went ashore and tried to talk to White Wolf, but he didn't want to talk, looking at Michael fearfully and with misgiving. Michael explained that a seventh son was deemed good medicine among the White folk and that they were honoured as healers. White Wolf would have none of it.

Michael told White Wolf that he had the bride price in his rowboat, but White Wolf said that he wouldn't accept it. Michael asked the older man if he would accept it as a gift. White Wolf declined.

Michael returned and fetched from the dory the gifts that he had for his brother-in-law, carrying each of the items up the shingle and placing them above high-water mark:

25 pounds rice,
50 pounds flour,

25 pounds white beans,
25 pounds yellow peas, split,
25 pounds prunes,
25 pounds dried apricots,
25 pounds dried apple,
5 sticks of pressed tobacco,
2 sugar loaves, wrapped in blue paper,
25 pounds of nails in a wooden box.

Also included was a package containing several lengths of cloth which was a gift from Maisie to her brother and his wife.

Michael then fetched a piece of old sail cloth which he placed over the mound, tied it securely, walked down the beach without looking backward or at any of the Native men silently watching from a distance, pushed off the dory, nimbly hopped in as if he were thirty years younger, and returned to the schooner.

Michael Locke, having exhausted his three days of visiting time, proceeded down the Labrador coast until, two days later, they reached Mercury Bight, a few miles south of Tumbler Bight, the location of the Oxford rooms. Because the harbour ice had not yet dispersed, he took advantage of the time to do on-shore repairs. His crew set about repairing the cook-shack, stages, bunk-houses and other structures necessary to prosecute the cod-fishery on that coast and to look after a crew of eight men.

What to do about Charles and Little Sparrow? All of his crew were, at least nominally, staunch Methodists, and although these men had no hesitation in welcoming an attractive maiden in their midst, they were adamant that the young couple could not sleep together unless they were married. He was also concerned about what might happen if one of the men took a fancy to the unmarried girl. She was comely! He didn't know whether she was naïve and whether "things" might happen while she remained on shore while Charles accompanied the skiff to the traps and trawls.

Consequently, on Thursday, he made the run north to Tumbler Tickle to discover that George Oxford had arrived on station the previous day. The result of his consultations with the recognized and almost universally respected Methodist lay-reader was that on Sunday, in the presence of whatever fishing crews were on station - and they were considerable - Charles Locke was married to Winifred, the name Charles chose for his young wife, on the deck of his father's schooner, officiated by George Oxford, assisted by his son, Francis, the latter about thirty years old..

The clerical fisherman, now showing his age (He was about 65 years old), holding a Master of Divinity from Oxford University and letters of ordination from some Unitarian group in England, explained to the assembled fisherman that a clergyman, of whatever description, does no more than acknowledge and witness a marriage, that it is God who did the joining of man and wife. There were nods of understanding all around although many of the men had never before heard that explanation of the marriage sacrament.

Later, while they were enjoying a cup of tea and partridgeberry pie, compliments of the cooks of the various ships now at anchor in the harbour, several of the Roman Catholics explained that they already had the understanding expounded by George Oxford, intelligence that several of their priests had provided over the years.

Little Sparrow, now Winifred, was now considered safe from marauding hands. She was a married woman. As such, no man dast even think lustfully after her. The marriage vow was sacred, ordained by God himself. They had witnessed the mystery.

They would no more dare to think carnally about the young woman than they would cut off their member with the fishing knife. It simply was not done. Whatever sin these men folk entertained in their hearts or committed by deed – and they might have been otherwise considerable - they came from a culture where adultery was virtually unknown, except as a taboo in the scriptures. Incest they might have known about; they were not angels or otherwise particularly virtuous, but actual adultery was unknown, unthinkable. Amorous exploits before marriage was accepted, even encouraged, and was not considered adultery. But, for a married man or woman to lie with another who was not their own bona fide spouse, was unthinkable.

For the remainder of the summer Little Sparrow laboured in the cook-house and at such other chores as the cook could find for her. She was admired by all for her industry and her gentle ways.

Michael, in order to give the young couple some privacy, gave up his cabin on the schooner and took a bunk in the bunkhouse. Charles and Little Sparrow had the captain's cabin to themselves.

By the end of August, it was obvious that the girl was bearing a child. Charles became the butt of numerous crude jokes, almost all of them reflecting negatively on his manhood and sexual prowess, virtually all of them suggesting that somebody else had done the deed. Charles weathered the onslaught in good grace, knowing that behind the ribald diatribe was a respect because he held his own in the trap-skiff and on the gutting line. That was where a man showed his mettle, and they all knew it.

The presence of this couple's association with Michael Locke's crew was a stroke of good fortune that these simple men could never have anticipated. Michael's being a seventh son had already proven its worth as far as these men were concerned. Ever since Michael had taken over as master from his father, their "vijes," - as the men called their voyages, the trips to the Labrador for fish - had been well above average.

Ever since young Charles joined the crew as unpaid apprentice about five years ago, their voyages had been even better. The power of the aura had even affected the other fishing crews who shared the harbour. For the past five or six years, there had been an increasing willingness for the various crews to keep their traps tied up with excess fish so that another crew, not having filled their day's hoped-for quota, would be able to top-up.

Now that a seventh son of a seventh son and a seventh daughter of a seventh daughter were there in the bight with them, these men, all of the men from all of the crews, felt that they would have a wonderful vije for sure. Even the cursed water pups - the sores on their wrists where the skin was rubbed raw from their fishing jackets, somehow seemed more bearable.

These simple and trusting men eagerly sought out Little Sparrow - the name that the men insisted on calling her - in order that she apply to their wrists a concoction of various greases and herbs that she had prepared. The grease came from a great white bear that had been killed in mid-June as well as from various geese and other birds that the cooks and their assistants had procured, a normal aspect of their functioning.

Little Sparrow was wont to go to the forests in search of herbs to include in her preparations, but the men made sure that she didn't go alone, several of them always ready to accompany her, each taking a gun in case some predator should happen to be lying in wait.

Moreover, even though she was not the only female in the cove, there being two other women from Newfoundland serving as cooks with other crews, she was revered, and almost every man in the bight thought of and spoke of her as a beloved sister. She was loved; her presence was a delight to these hardened men.

The summer passed as summers do on the Labrador coast, with the normal compliment of storms, with the normal compliment of men accidentally toppling into the frigid water. However, there were no deaths. How could there be? There in that bight were three people embodying the most powerful mysteries these men could fathom - a seventh son, his seventh son and the seventh of a seventh daughter. Never had these men been so richly blessed. Even when they attended George Oxford's Sunday afternoon divine services over at Tumbler Bight, the spirit of the Lord seemed to shine on them all the more because of the presence of these three people.

When the fully laden schooner sailed into Little Bay Islands harbour last Saturday of October, Charles holding Little Sparrow's hand, the men who lived in the village each found an excuse to stand near the young couple and to point out to the maiden the house where his family lived. She nodded graciously, overwhelmed with the size of the village. Other than the summer fishing villages that she had visited, populated almost solely by men and consisting of rather crudely constructed buildings of various kinds, all functional in the fishery, this was the largest community that she had ever seen. She hadn't anticipated even the White folk having towns so large.

She looked thoughtfully at her husband, her hands now protectively over her prominent belly, Charles' arm over her shoulder. Would his people accept her as the fishermen had done? Would she be welcomed? Would she feel at home? What kind of home would she have?

Little Sparrow gave birth to a man child near the end of March, 1871, barely six weeks before Charles had to leave her to return to the Labrador. They had spent the winter with Michael and Maisie, the latter being her proper aunt. She felt loved and a part of the family.

Charles, however, had suggested that they not build a house at Little Bay Islands, but at a small sheltered cove on the neighbouring island where there were already three or four families. It was merely a mile and a half, or so, almost directly south of Suley Ann's Cove, the cove on the southern side of Little Bay Islands of the island where several families resided. It wasn't a matter of Charles having any dispute with his neighbours or that he would not have preferred to live in his natal village.

The issue was that there was an extremely inadequate amount of arable land on that small island. On the neighbouring island, Sunday Cove Island, particularly at Welman's Cove where he had proposed to Winifred that they live, there was sufficient land available that would allow the family to grow a sufficient quantity of potatoes, turnips, carrot, and cabbage to meet their needs during the long winter months. Winifred had never known anything about growing vegetables and was excited at the prospect and at learning new skills. Moreover, Charles was going to acquire some sheep and a cow. Winifred would have a lot of learning to do!

September, 1873, Winifred gave birth to a girl but it died at birth. Actually, according to the dictates of the times, the child had a deformity and the midwife did what she was supposed to do.

August, 1875, baby girl number three made its appearance. It initially thrived, but died before Charles arrived home from the Labrador.

In September, 1876, another girl was delivered to the family. Initially sickly, she rallied and became quite healthy. Her great great grandchildren still live in the area.

Early in October, 1878, a week before Charles arrived home from the Labrador fishery, girl number five saw the first light of day. The child thrived.

The news that the blessed couple had now brought five girls in succession into the world became the talk of the bay. Was it possible that there could be a seventh girl. The seventh daughter of a seventh of seventh daughter and of the seventh of a seventh son? What awesome powers such a person would have!

Early in November, 1881, girl child number six made her appearance. She thrived.

Even grizzled old fishing captains were talking about the possibilities inherent in a seventh daughter of the couple. That she would have awesome powers, there would be no doubt. But, would these powers be used for good or for ill? It was such an unusual circumstance, the first ever in their knowledge, they really didn't know what to expect. Anticipation was palpable, but the fear was not well hidden.

When Charles left for the Labrador in May, 1883, the word was abroad that Winifred was already big with child. Would it be a boy or a girl. Even a boy should have impressive powers. But a seventh girl!

All the Methodist churches in the bay had special prayers for the health of the mother and baby. The people supposed that if the child was born after a season of prayer for its welfare and salvation, it would not bode ill for the people. Or ... would it?

152

Tales from Harbour Divine
The Oral and Folk Story Tradition Of Western Notre Dame Bay,
north east coast of Newfoundland Island

Maisie, now well up in her sixties, had gone across the bay to assist at the birth of the grandchild. She, too, was worried. This would have been an auspicious occasions for her tribe, but she couldn't push away the sense of foreboding she felt because of the seventh sonship of the baby's father and grandfather, neither of whom would have survived the first minute of birth had they been born to her Labrador people. She couldn't push away the anxiety.

She later revealed to Michael that her over-riding concern, the one that led her to be present at the birth, was that the midwife was known to dispatch defectives rather efficiently. In fact, there had been some concern that, on several occasions, she might have gotten carried away with her zeal to keep pure the bloodlines of the people. Did, for example, an extra toe constitute a defect that warranted death for the child? Virtually everyone in the bay agreed that a devil child or a child with obvious deformities had no right to live, that it should die before it cried and called, simply, a still birth. Although it wasn't a topic that was regularly discussed, it was a principle of life by common consent, a matter of pragmatics. But an extra toe?

Although concerns might sometimes be whispered, few people were prepared to intervene with a mid-wife's decisions. It was a weight that these people gladly placed on the shoulders of the mid-wife and off their own. For some people, there might, sometimes, be some small niggling but unarticulated concern about certain moral and ethical issues. But for a people generally without education and steeped in mythology-integrated religion, they left such weighty matters to their betters. It was not proper for people to strive above their station and, clearly, such issues had already been decided appropriate by people occupying the higher rungs of society. Who were they to dispute such matters?

Maisie was concerned that the midwife's zeal might extend to issues that had nothing to do with physical deformities. Maisie knew that the midwife also had Labrador ancestry and continued to live by the pragmatics, values, and cultural beliefs of her distant ancestors, the pragmatics which helped her ancestral tribes survive. Because Maisie did not know for sure where the midwife's sentiments lay with respect to the mythology surrounding seventh children, she was not prepared to leave certain decisions to the woman. If the child were a girl and if it had no obvious deformities, than Maisie would make sure that the child lived.

She felt that her fears were well-founded when the midwife told her that she didn't want Maisie to assist at the birth. Maisie held her ground. The midwife said that she would go home. Maisie told her to go on, that she, Maisie, was quite capable of helping a child into the world.

At last, no doubt fearing that she would lose her fifty cent fee for assisting at the birth, the midwife relented. She grumbled about not being allowed to do her job, but she relented.

The girl-child was born mid-September: A beautiful little tyke, brown, chubby, jet-black hair, and killing eyes. The midwife declared that the girl was a witch child - those eyes, those eyes! - and should die immediately. Maisie refused, saying that if the mid-wife laid a malevolent hand on the child, she, Maisie, would dispatch the midwife. The midwife refused to touch either mother or child, immediately left the house, shouting her curses and declaring to the other folks of the village that a demon had been born among them.

Had it not been for Alexander Wellman, an old Labrador fisherman who could hardly hobble about, it is anyone's guess what might have happened. That old Methodist, assisted by a fearful grand-daughter, came to the house and, violating village custom, knocked at the door. He had come, he said, to baptize the child. The people were fearful. But their fears would be alleviated if the child were baptized and washed in holy water.

Thus, barely three hours old, the child was washed in water that Mr, Wellman read scriptures over, prayed over, and then blessed. Then, the old man called on the Almighty to reveal his presence and to bless the child and accept her as one of His children.

Whether the girl might have been a witch-child or not, we will never know. Whatever malevolent forces might have been surrounding the infant, they were surely dispelled by Mr. Wellman's prayers, his Bible reading, and his blessings.

The child was called Purity.

Charles arrived home third week of October. The following Sunday morning, he, his wife, his three older daughters, and virtually all of the other residents of Wellman's Cove sailed across the bay to Sully Ann's Cove, walked across the brow to The Methodist church and, before a full congregation, delivered his seventh daughter more formally to the Lord.

The minister baptized the girl again, received her into the body of Christ, and reaffirmed her name. After his prayer of thanksgiving, there was so much hub-hub in the church that the parson could hardly preach his morning sermon. He had hardly pronounced the benediction when the congregation surged forward. Everybody wanted to catch a glimpse of the child. People put out their hands to reverently touch the child's head. They returned to their humble cottages feeling that they had witnessed a special phenomenon, that they had been blessed.

But the eyes!

The baby's eyes!

Everyone commented on the girl's eyes.

The baby had been alert all morning, all through the service, hadn't even cried when she had the sign of the cross made on her forehead by the baptismal water. When people came to see and touch her, she had gazed intently and intensely back at them.

What colour were the eyes? People couldn't say. Black? Green? The blinding liquid silver of the sun? The colour of the deep sea?

Whatever the colour, everyone on whom the girl's gaze fell declared that they could feel the girl's looking at their inner being. "She looked right through me!" they said, in many variations of the sentiment. "She saw all of my sins!" said some more.

Charles and Winifred returned to Welman's Cove and settled in for the winter. They secured their harvested vegetables in the root cellar, killed one of the rams, and caught autumn cod out

156

Tales from Harbour Divine
The Oral and Folk Story Tradition Of Western Notre Dame Bay,
north east coast of Newfoundland Island

in the bay and sufficient dried for winter before the permanent snows came.

Purity thrived. She was the focus of the house. Her older sisters, as well as her proud parents, doted on her.

Despite the difficulty of travel, the Locke home had numerous visitors. People sailed across the bay from as far away as Western Arm on the north side of Green Bay, just to gaze on the wondrous child. Even the frozen ocean didn't stop them. People came from Long Island and Pilley's Island as well as from overland on snowshoes, from Miles Cove and Port Anson, and even as far away as Boot Harbour and Roberts Arm and up in Halls Bay, just to set eyes on the child.

Because Charles had to go back to little Bay Islands in March, to go in collar in preparation for the summer's fishery and to begin the process of taking over as master from his father who was now ailing, he took Winifred and the girls along and installed them in his parent's old house. The arrangement gave the older girls an opportunity to spend a little time at the village school, there being no school at Wellman's cove.

As soon as the ice broke up in April, the normal flurry of shipping activity commenced. Several hundred fishing masters from around the bay were "dealers" with Strong's Bros, the outfitting and provender firm centered at Little Bay Islands. At times, it was said, one could go across the ample harbour of Little Bay Islands from schooner deck to schooner deck, from one extremity to the other. Some fishermen declared that the harbour of Little Bay Islands was decked over, such was the number of fishing schooners there to pick up supplies.

Then a new phenomenon occurred.

The fishing masters began to make a pilgrimage to the Locke home, all wanting to see, to touch, the infant goddess. Grizzled and hardened men who had not been to church for forty years wended their way in their humility to gaze on the beautiful child.

Nobody knew quite who started the practice, but some said it was Garf Parsons, that rough and tumble man whom some wished would die because he was so "hard." Garf Parsons, at least, even if he were not the first, knelt by the child's cradle. The innocent eyes of the babe looked through the gruff exterior, looked beyond the blackness of soul and found a tender spot. The otherwise cruel and crude man tenderly reached forth his gnarled and tar-spattered hand, took the child's hand in his, bowed his head and placed the child's hand to his forehead. Gently releasing the baby's hand, the man began to weep.

The man was changed! His crew watched in amazement as, still weeping, he returned to his ship and secluded himself in his cabin. That summer, it was said, Garf Parsons was one of the best captains one could hope to work for on the Labrador coast.

Other captains made their visits, so much so that the parents were concerned for the welfare of the child. But, they waited their turn, and tried not to impose overly much. It was said that there was not a single fishing captain, in the spring of 1884, who did not visit the child before embarking on the run north to the Labrador.

The phenomenon repeated itself the following spring, except that now, the men were bringing gifts to the child. Several of the

158

Tales from Harbour Divine
The Oral and Folk Story Tradition Of Western Notre Dame Bay, north east coast of Newfoundland Island

men even went so far as to ask the child to forgive them. That un-nerved the mother. She mentioned it to Charles, but he didn't know what to do about it since no harm seemed to be done. The Methodist parson, however, preached on idolatry and let it be known that he disapproved of the practice.

As was their wont, the couple always attended the Methodist services when they were at Little Bay Islands. Typically, the baby was a focus of attention. People wanted to hold her, to kiss her, to touch her.

The years passed. Charles and Winifred stayed at Wellman's Cove from November to February. Winifred returned to their home at the end of May, planted vegetables, looked after her girls, and enjoyed the solitude of the cove and the neighborliness of the four other families.

In the summer, after Purity was seven years old, that is in 1890, the Methodist parson from Long Island visited the Locke household at Wellman's Cove and asked if Winifred and her daughters would care to visit the church at Lushes Bight or Cutwell Arm. His congregations had repeatedly made the request. Winifred said that she would ask Charles as soon as he returned in October. Not happy with the response, but having no other option, the minister went away.

Charles, not wishing to offend, on his return from the Labrador, sent a couple of lads across the bay to Lushes Bight with a letter for the minister: weather permitting, the family would cross the bay to Lushes Bight, a distance of less than six miles, second Sunday of November, and would return Monday morning, providing accommodations could be provided from Sunday night. They would attend services at both villages.

The churches were filled to capacity. The new portable pipe organ at Lushes Bight never sounded so sweet, folk said, and surely the bell never tolled so long.

Invitations to dinner were numerous and there was no shortage of offers to cart the family across the brow to Cutwell Arm in time for evening service.

Although the family received numerous invitations from as faraway as the Church of England congregation at Leading Tickles to Methodist churches well up in Green Bay, the family accepted no other such invitations. Ten or twenty miles were distances that one traveled only in emergency and only with favourable winds. The bay was treacherous, some said, even at the best of times.

As Purity grew, however, another phenomenon began to manifest. People who were ill began to find their way to the Locke home requesting that the girl pray for them. Pregnant women came and requested that the girl place her hand on their belly.

At first, the child was puzzled, not comprehending what people wanted from her. Eventually, however, she would repeat the Lord's Prayer with them and, if they requested, place her little hand on their heads. These people went away happy and declared that even if they weren't healed, the girl's blessing had helped them. The women with child declared that their childbirths were easier.

160

Tales from Harbour Divine
The Oral and Folk Story Tradition Of Western Notre Dame Bay,
north east coast of Newfoundland Island

It was probably in Purity's seventh or eighth year that other stories began to circulate. Charles attempted to suppress them, but could not deny them.

It seems that Purity was playing outside in the summer of 1891 when her next older sister ran to her mother and told her that Purity was playing with a strange dog. Winifred hastened to the window and looked out to see the little girl offering her hands to an enormous wolf. The girl had just had a slice of molasses bread. The animal was licking molasses from the girl's outstretched hand. Winifred froze. What should she do?

She hastened outside but stopped. The large animal had lain on his back and the girl was rubbing his tummy. Seeing Winifred, the wolf leapt up and hastened toward the forest. Winifred ran and snatched up the unharmed girl, trying to decide if she should to scold her unusual daughter - but scold her for what?

It had become common knowledge that birds would congregate around the girl. Jays were regular visitors; Sparrows and Tom Tits and Foxy Furkers and Robins went about their business of seeking worms and grubs within a few feet of her, seeming to have no fear of her, even seeming to welcome her presence. Even Crows and Gulls and Sterrins would come and maintain vigilance on nearby fence posts and rails, looking at her, seeming to want to be in her presence.

In the autumn of 1891, shortly after Charles had come home from the Labrador, he was finishing his dinner when he heard Winifred gasp. He hurried to the window. Purity was holding out her hands to a Lynx, calling, "Here kitty, here pussy." The big cat readily approached her. Charles grabbed his gun from its cradle over the stove and began to load it. Winifred, however, delayed him and said to watch. They watched in fascination as the big cat allowed Purity to ruffle its fur. Then it lay by her as she rubbed its belly. After a few minutes, the cat got to its feet, licked her face, and ambled into the forest.

As soon as the animal had gone, the parents rushed out. The older girls said that the cat was a regular visitor, that Purity had been feeding it since early summer.

The summer of Purity's eleventh year was one that her mother would talk about until she died, at age approximately 76, in 1931. She said that the family of girls and herself were seated around the supper table on a bright evening around the first week of July. Discussion ranged through those items of interest to the girls: wondering how their dad was doing, he having been gone for almost two months and at least another three months before they would see him again; dolls' cloths; new dresses; a boy who was visiting the Wellman family from across the bay, and so on.

Purity, out of the blue, said, "I played with the little people, today."

There was a shocked silence as her sisters stared at her and then at their mother. Winifred, also, stared at her precocious daughter, not knowing what to say. Was the girl being deceptive? Was she sick?

Although fairies was a topic of intermittent conversation throughout the bay, along with witches, tokens, and various and sundry other signs, shades and spiritual phenomena, Winifred had never met anybody who had actually seen one. Moreover, the little people of her own tribal myths seemed not to have a presence among these people.

"Little people?" She asked her question gently. "Where did you see them?"

"Over by the birch trees, on the other side of the yard, pass the potato beds."

"What were they doing?"

"They came and played with me. They formed a ring around me and played and sang something like *Ring around a rosie.*"

"Did you understand what they were saying?"

"No, Mamma. Don't be silly. I don't understand their language. But they were laughing and driving works with each other."

"Only boys?"

Winifred asked the question because the myths of her people only ever mentioned male little people. She could not recall ever hearing about female little people.

"Boys and girls, Mamma. And they all had colourful clothes on."

Winifred again had reason to be surprised because the little people of her ancestral myths only ever mentioned little men who were covered with their own fur or, otherwise, were wearing skins of squirrels or mice or rabbit.

"Well, don't let them be leading you into the woods, mind, now." The warning coming out of the local mythology that fairies used to lead people astray.

On two other occasions that summer Purity mentioned, matter of factly, that she had again seen the little people.

Although she never again saw whatever it was that she saw, even when she was several years older, up to her final months, Purity would always insist that she had seen the little people the summer that she was eleven.

As Purity grew older, she began to understand what people wanted of her and she was eager to oblige. Boats were continually arriving in the cove from various villages around the bay, from as far as twenty miles away which, given the reality of transportation over open ocean around a treacherous seacoast, was a long distance. Charles and Winifred tried unsuccessfully to quell the demand, but earned the wrath of their neighbours in the surrounding villages. If Purity had "the gift" of healing, or at least, soothing pain, then she should be providing it. This was an era when doctors were unknown. If people became ill, thy died.

Curiously, there seemed to be little solid expectation that Purity would actually heal a person or prevent one from dying, although there were a few persons who made such claims. However, what Purity was capable of doing, or so it was claimed, was ease a person's pain and provide a dying person with an easier transition to the great beyond.

Charles, spending six months of the year away from home, namely being on the Labrador coast prosecuting the annual

164

Tales from Harbour Divine
The Oral and Folk Story Tradition Of Western Notre Dame Bay,
north east coast of Newfoundland Island

fishery, was hardly in a position to assist his wife in controlling the activities of his growing daughter. He did, however, put his foot down, and say that Purity would not be permitted to travel over bad ice.

Even so, people from as far away as Pilley's Island and Three Arms were requesting the ministrations of the maiden and were sending dog teams after her to come and pray with someone who was dying or otherwise experiencing a birth trauma. Charles and Winifred were exhausted by all the comings and goings. Purity, however, seemed to enjoy the experience and appeared to be thriving on the attention. Although many people had pressed gifts on her, her father had taught her that if she was indeed doing good work, then she couldn't accept anything but nominal gifts. Otherwise, the nature of her power might be misconstrued and misunderstood. Suggestions of witchcraft still, occasionally, raised its ugly head.

April, 1897, was a more or less normal year in the western reaches of Notre Dame Bay. Although there had been several late-winter storms, the bay ice had held, at least the ice in between the islands. Most people, however, were now exercising caution. Even seemingly solid expanses of ice could be hiding swatches, areas where upwellings and tides had eaten away the ice from underneath and where an unwary step could send one into the frigid depths.

Ocean ice is especially treacherous in another way. Freshwater ice is brittle and has a hard edge which might make it efficacious in clambering back to the surface of the ice should one happen to break through and fall into the water. In contrast, saltwater ice is flexible. If one breaks through and tumbles into the water, the edge of the ice is likely to bend and get wet and slippery, making it extremely difficult, if not impossible, for the unfortunate person to succeed in pulling himself up to the surface. The other difficulty, if one happens to fall into the ocean water between flows of so-called "rough ice" – that is pieces of Arctic ice – is that if one manages to grasp a piece of ice, it tends to tip over in order to maintain its equilibrium, a completely normal and understandable physical phenomenon. In short, ocean ice can be treacherous.

The residents of the villages of the north east coast of the island of Newfoundland were always wary of traveling over ocean ice and did so only reluctantly and usually taking particular precautions such as traveling with a companion who kept some distance away, taking ropes, taking a small boat on one's kometik, and so on. Moreover, if at all possible, one did not travel at night nor immediately after a snowstorm. Snow can cover open water and make it appear to be solid ice.

Purity was almost fourteen years old. She now understood quite well what people wanted of her and she was happy to respond to their requests. She discovered that her touch on a hot forehead seemed to bring immense comfort to the afflicted; a hand on the belly of a pregnant woman seemed to make the birth easier; a prayer with a dying person seemed to bring much comfort and enabled the person to die peacefully. These were uneducated people with a simple Christian faith inextricably interwoven and tangled up with all sorts of superstitions and folk magic.

166

Tales from Harbour Divine
*The Oral and Folk Story Tradition Of Western Notre Dame Bay,
north east coast of Newfoundland Island*

This was an era when people still believed in ghosts, people still saw fairies, where tokens were a regularly experienced phenomenon and witches lived in almost every village. To believe in the powers of a seventh son and especially the seventh of a seventh was as natural as breathing. These people suckled these folk beliefs with their mother's milk. Moreover, most of these people had aboriginal ancestry and brought the beliefs of their ancestral folk with them when they made the transition to more or less outport village life. It would be difficult to say exactly where European based folk belief left off and Aboriginal folk belief took on. They became intertwined and of a piece. The sets of beliefs had combined to become a whole.

Thus it was, in April of 1897, Aunt Carrie Oxford, 86 years old, lay dying. She knew she was dying; her family knew she was dying. Aunt Carrie wasn't afraid to die. She had lived as Christian all her life, Christian of the Unitarian-tinged Wesleyan Methodist variety, tempered by the folk belief of her Beothuck mother. As she laboured to breathe, she whispered, "Wooden it be wonnerful if that good girl, that beautiful Purity, cood come and pray with me!"

The implicit request was immediately passed to Gabriel and Robert, her two middle aged sons. Thus, they readied their dog team and prepared to go across the bay to fetch Purity.

As the team came down through Francis Oxford's garden in Sully Ann's Cove, they stopped momentarily to greet their cousin.

"Where you off to, dis marnin, gentmn?"

"Goin across the Bay, Skipper, ta fetch Purity fer Mother."

"Bies, da bay's not safe. I'm advisin' ya not ta go."

"Naw, Farncis, Sure we've ad hard frost. She's sa solied as in da middle a da winter."

"Don't think so. I seed the ice move yestiddy. I think you'm on a fool's errand. Tis too dangerous, I tell you."

"Mother's dyin. She wants Purity."

"Yes, I knows yer mother's dyin. I kin understand why she wants Purity. But tis too dangerous, I tell you. Let me come back wit ya and pray fer yer mother."

"Francis, we knows you'm a good man and a godly man and we respects ya fer yer work in da church and bein lay reader an all dat. You can still come ta pray with Mother. But, right now she wants Purity. So, we'm goin after Purity."

"Den put my rodney on yet kometik. Da hice is too treacherous, I tell you. Jis look at the pressure ridges. Dey've farmed taday!"

Thurza, Francis Oxford's seventeen year old daughter, was standing by the door listening to the conversation between the men. She sort of hoped that the men would go fetch Purity. She liked the younger maiden and anticipated that the latter would visit with them if she came across to Little Bay Islands. She remembered the day vividly, even fifty years later.

Unable to dissuade the two men, Francis Oxford bade them be careful and wished them well. He came into the kitchen shaking his head. "I don't think they'll make it. Tis foolish, tis foolish, tis foolhardy."

168

Tales from Harbour Divine
The Oral and Folk Story Tradition Of Western Notre Dame Bay,
north east coast of Newfoundland Island

Francis Oxford watched from his window as the men took to the windswept ice. He watched as they made their way across the mile and a half, weaving between the pressure ridges, the latter phenomenon a sure sign that the ice had weakened. He watched as the dog team and kometik gained the far shore. He continued to watch.

The pressure ridges!

The issue was talked about for years afterward. The pressure ridges, as the term implies, indicated (a) that the ice was under extreme pressure and (b) the ice had weakened. Pressure ridges in the middle of the winter were one thing; pressure ridges in late winter or early spring constituted another matter entirely. There was not a man or youth alive, over the age of fifteen years, at Little Bay Islands or in any of the surrounding villages who did not understand the danger implicit in the appearance of these upheavals of bay ice. They spelled danger. Only under extreme duress would anyone venture out on the bay ice under the prevalent conditions. At least, the Oxford men shuld have taken a rodney or other small boat, just in case, as did some men even on the self-same day who were out "swatchin", that is "swiling" - shooting seals who were using the swatches as blowing holes.

A half hour after the dog team had gained the opposite shore, Francis Oxford watched as a group of people left the Locke residence at Wellman's Cove. He watched as the team left the shore and headed back across the bay.

When they were about half way across, more or less, he saw the team stop. He saw the two men race to the dogs. He saw an ice pan flip. He saw some floundering. Then, all was still. The ice was empty, being swept by the wind.

Neither the dog team nor the kometik nor the bodies of Gabriel and Robert Oxford were ever seen again, two women and nine children left widowed and fatherless, left to fend for themselves in that brutal environment.

As if Nature itself wished to press home the foolhardiness of the quest on which the men ventured, even before duckish had set in, a swell had developed and the wind had swung around to the south west, thus deterring any of the men who were now milling around on the shore at Suley Ann's Cove, with their dog teams and kometics at the ready, trying to decide whether to temp the fates even more and to venture out across what they now knew to be rotten ice. The heaving of the ice and the freshening wind was all the warming they needed. Nobody left the shore, although they maintained vigil until well after midnight, the men taking turn by twos and threes to visit Francis and Emma Oxford's kitchen to be fortified by strong tea and a hunk of hot molasses bread.

By midnight, they knew the game was up. They could hear the ice moving, even if they were not able to see through the later winter gloom.

Next morning, when Francis Oxford got up at dawn and lit the fire in his fireplace, he looked across the bay. No ice was visible. All that could be seen was the blackish green choppy water . The bay ice had been broken up by the swell and had been dispersed on the wide North Atlantic by the sou-west winds. Although the bay would eventually fill again with rough ice, that is Arctic ice, within a week or so and would remain until late May, the bay ice, the traveling ice, was gone for another year.

During the summer, some bedlamer boys were jigging for squids off Copper Island, one of the small islands midway between Suley Ann's Cove and Wellman's Cove. A jigger snagged something heavy. The boys, hearts pounding in anticipation and fear, knowing what might be at the end of their line, slowly and reluctantly pulled in their line. They discovered a home made quilt, breaching in the turbulent ocean water. They pulled the humble artifact into their boat and made their way back to the harbour. Eventually, the humble homemade blanket was identified by Winifred as the quilt that she had wrapped around Purity as she had settled on the kometik on that fateful day.

No other remnants of the girl or any article of her clothing were ever seen again.

THE END

Acknowledgments:

The essence of this story was related on numerous occasions to numerous visitors by Thirza Anthony (nee: Locke-Oxford), although the story might have varied slightly with each telling, as such stories always do, and maybe should. The major aspect of the story occurred when she was a girl growing up at Suley Ann's Cove on Little Bay Islands. The Locke family was her mother's; the George Oxford mentioned in the story was her grandfather; Francis was her father.

172

Tales from Harbour Divine
*The Oral and Folk Story Tradition Of Western Notre Dame Bay,
north east coast of Newfoundland Island*

The Last Veteran of Harbour Divine

Newfoundland and Labrador is proud of its military veterans, all those men and women who offered to make the supreme sacrifice, offering to lay down their lives for their country. We cherish them and we have numerous ceremonies and functions in which to honour them. It is especially gratifying to them when schools invite them to functions and give them the opportunity to wear their medals, medallions, ribbons and other regalia. Children idolize them and, given the opportunity, will write stories and poems and create all sorts of art work in their honour. That is as it should be.

Harbour Divine has had at least several dozen veterans – First World War, Second World War, Korea, for example. At one time, there were even two old codgers who were veterans of the Boar War – they had even been regimental buddies - and could tell many stories about their experiences in South and central Africa and how they fell in love with Kaffir girls. Several dozen young men went through boot camp at several military bases across Canada, and some served as exchange soldiers with the American and British Forces. Harbour Divine boys – and in later years, several girls - served in all branches – naval, land and air – and in a bewildering variety of occupations and trades. Many of them have, quite deservingly, received commendations, service

Tales from Harbour Divine
The Oral and Folk Story Tradition Of Western Notre Dame Bay,
north east coast of Newfoundland Island

173

medals, honour for valour, and so on. More recently, we have a new crop of veterans, men and women, career soldiers, who have served all across the globe, with NATO, the UN, and otherwise. Now some of them are still overseas, still serving their country, and Harbour Divine is still proud of its own.

Harbour Divine has had its share of genuine heros. Alas, some of them didn't return to tell us their stories. The humble cairn over on the hill near the Orange Hall lists about two dozen young men who went off in 1914 and didn't return. The loss was great! Only three of Harbour Divine's sons returned from that great conflagration. Jessie Burches was a decorated navel veteran and came home badly wounded. He never worked again and died before he was thirty. James Belfalon was in the July Drive and came home with only one leg. The other is still over there in France, somewhere. James learned Morse Code and served as telegraph operator and Harbour Divine post master until in the early 1950s when he took honourable retirement. He died around 1963. Franklyn Boylman went through the war unscathed, stayed home for a year or so afterward, then went off to the US where he studied engineering. He became quite wealthy, apparently, and died just a few years ago at age 98. But, he returned to Harbour Divine for a visit almost every summer.

Almost all of these veterans were members of the local Canadian Legion - closed, now, because there are not a sufficient number of veterans remaining to keep it going. The building was torn down and the new Harbour Divine Town Hall has been constructed on the site. There is a plaque in the foyer listing all known veterans of the military and police forces whose origin was

Harbour Divine or who lived at Harbour Divine at some time or other.

Most of Harbour Divine's veterans were only too pleased to oblige when they were asked to participate in community events. One veteran, however, William Twilling, never ever responded to letters inviting him to participate or, if asked by telephone or in person, always found an excuse not to be involved - either he had prior commitments, or he was going to be away for work, or he was sick, or one of his youngsters was sick, or his wife was sick, or he had do some work for the church, or .... He had an endless list of excuses. Many people said that they could not understand why he would not participate, Willie being a hero and all. Other residents of the village, however, were sympathetic and claimed to understand. William must have had some rather traumatic experiences during his term of war service, and any such gathering would serve only to remind him of them. Some people said that he was still suffering from *shell shock*, now called PTSD.

It was not a matter of William not being able to accommodate crowds, now. William was a active member of the local Methodist Church and loved to conduct the evening after service. Yes, yes, it is the United Church, now, but that is merely a name. The United Church at Harbour Divine as a body corporate, as a gathering of like-minded people, is Methodist, Unitarian-Wesleyan Methodist, mind, in their thought, behaviour (or lack thereof), beliefs and tithing (or lack thereof!). As such, they believed strongly - still do - in the priesthood of the laity, and the laity, as William Twilling did, still have lots of opportunity to exercise their priesthood, their membership in the Priesthood of Melchizadech. In that sense,

William Twilling was a priest whom most of the congregation recognized as such.

Now, William Twilling, known by most of his work mates as Willie or simply Will, was not, otherwise, an unreasonable man. He was personable, gentle, kind, funny, witty, helpful, hard-working, religious, respectful to his wives (serially, of course), gentle with his children. Although not well educated, he was known to be intelligent and logical. Although not argumentative, if Willie had a fault it was regarding his religion. He was not terribly open-minded as far as religion was concerned. Willie had been born Methodist, Unitarian-Wesleyan Methodist, mind you, and he had determined that his version of Methodism was the only religion a reasonable man might be.

Even though religious, Willie was no prude, and he despised those who "let their religion get the better of them," so he said. If they couldn't laugh and make a joke, Willie was quick to classify them as "sour," regardless of religious persuasion – or lack thereof, because he observed that sourness was not characteristic of only those who attended some or other church. He was wont to say, "Be d'way dey walks around so sour-lookin' you'd tink dey 'ad a turd hanging under deir noses."

Willie was musical and loved to play the button accordion and mouth organ. He was always one of the first to get a group of people together to go singing the Christmas or New year's carol and, until his late sixties, he was still eager to go jannying.

Will had memorized a prodigious amount of poetry, a characteristic he shared with several other residents of the village.

176

Tales from Harbour Divine
The Oral and Folk Story Tradition Of Western Notre Dame Bay,
north east coast of Newfoundland Island

It was the one attribute upon which virtually all of the community agreed that constituted a larned man - or woman.   Although there might not have been any overt competition for memorizing the most or the longest poems, if a book was discovered whose contents was poetry, then it was lent and borrowed around the village until those who prided themselves on their store of memorized poetry had had their way with the tome. Several people, mostly men - who, presumably had more time for such intellectual pursuits - claimed to have memorized hundreds of poems, almost all of them beginning with the poetry of Number One Royal Reader. If any man couldn't recite - maybe, somewhat enviously - a simple poem such as *The Miller of the Dee,* then he was considered a Philistine, indeed!

That particular poem seems to have been brought to Notre Dame Bay by the earliest West Country immigrants. There are several extant versions and adaptations, one of which follows:

The Miller of the Dee

There was a jolly miller once,
Lived near the river Dee;
He worked and sang from more til night,
No lark so blithe as he.
And this the burden of his song
Forever used to be:
I care for nobody, no not I,
If nobody cares for me.

The reason why he was so blithe,
He once did thus unfold:
The bread I eat my hands have earn'd;
I covet no man's gold;
I do not fear next squaring-day;
In debt to none I be.
I care for nobody, no, not I,
If nobody cares for me.

A coin or two I've in my purse,
To help a needy friend ;
A little I can give the poor,
And still have some to spend.
Though I may fail, yet I rejoice,
Another's good luck to see.
I care for nobody, no, not I,
If nobody cares for me.

So let us his example take,
And be from malice free;
Let every one his neighbour serve,
As served he'd like to be.
And merrily pass the jug about
And drink and sing with glee;
If nobody cares a tittle for us,
Why not a jot care we.

There are numerous versions of this poem, the original seemingly composed by Isaac Bickerstaffe in 1762 and included in his composition, *Love in a Village.*

Willie began memorizing poems from the time he was a mere lad. There were in fact, few sources of poetry in the village - *The Royal Readers, The Royal Crown Readers,* and other school books. The local mechant, Nhimsheiaha Hewlett, a veteran of WWI, had a small library and used to borrow books from his cousin, Adolphus Hewlett who lived at Beaver Arm, way over on the other side of the bay. The one other source of books was the library at the manse of the Methodist parson. (It was well up in the fifties before the people got around to calling their clergyman the United Church minister!)

Some of the poems in Willie's memory consisted of sixty or seventy verses. One of his favourites was *The Orangemen's Alphabet* which has thirty verses. Willie had gone to the Labrador for a number of summers after the war with the Ryans from Pilley's Island, learned whatever they knew, and loved to recite some of the poems and doggreal from that village. One such poem commemorated how a sick woman had to be treated by

the doctor, there being a Grenfell hospital at Pilley's Island from
1911 to 1916:

> Jasper Reid and Samuel Locke
> Come all the way from Spencer's Dock
> The Boys from Holy Hole did flock
> Shake up yer wagon, Furey.
>
> Dolly Maddocks from Spencer's Hill
> She is sick and very Ill
> Doctor, doctor, try your skill
> Hurry Doctor Chambers.
>
> All the men out on Belle Isle
> Goes out fishin' once a while
> Trims their lamps with kerosene oil
> Paddy, you'm a karker!

Moreover, Will loved to sing. He was always singing. Some
people suggested it was to get out of his mind some of the horrific
experiences of the war. He used to give an outstanding rendition
of "Way over Yonder on the Hilltop".

Way Over Yonder on the Hilltop

*There's goin' to be a glorious time by-and-by
Way over yonder on the hilltop
Where the moon shines bright in the cloudless sky
Way over yonder on the hilltop!
At that great camp meeting we'll work no more
we'll play a little tune on the old banjo,
And de bells keep a ringing on the golden shore.
Way over yonder on the hilltop!*

*CHORUS: Way over yonder where da children am a singing,
And de bells keep ringing,
Way over yonder on the hilltop.
Take de narrow little railroad smooth and straight,
Way over yonder on the hilltop!
If you travel by the broad gauge you'll sure to be late,
Way over yonder on the hilltop!*

*You fashionable people with your pomp and pride,
all painted up and powdered and your hair all dyed,
Like the label on the bottle, you'll be left outside.
Way over yonder on the hilltop!   Chorus:*

When Gabriel blows his silver horn,
Way over yonder on the hilltop!
Get you ready for to travel in the early morn,
Way over yonder on the hilltop!
But you needn't come along if you don't look neat,
You must throw dem worldly shoes from off your feet,
Or dey'll never let you walk in the golden streets
Way over yonder on the hilltop!   *Chorus:*

It was understood by the people of Pilley's Island and, consequently, by Willie, that some unknown resident of that village - such as Jasper Whalen of Bumblbee Bight, now long dead - had composed the song. The villagers believed that this was the origin of the song because it had been sung by generations of the people, there, and in other villages in the bay.

[Actually the song was composed by a Black freed slave from the southern United States by the name of William Mallory who had been quite a successful military officer rising to the rank of colonel. He wrote the song about 1860. How this song became so popular, and "owned" by the people of western Notre Dame Bay is still a mystery. (The version given above is the Pilley's Island version, not the original Southern version in which, for example, b replaced the v.) It was quit the search to discover the original. However, apparently, there is one copy existing of the book in which this poem appears, now preserved in the Rare Book Room of the University of Virginia.]

Another of Will's favourite songs was Ira Stanphill's *Mansion over the Hilltop,* and when he led the witness time in the Methodist after-services, he would, almost inevitably, begin with that old spiritual. (The Mansion over the Hilltop is still in copyright).

But probably Willie's trademark song was The Drinking House Over the Way, written by some unknown tragic soul, a song that he memorized from one of the numerous religious tracts that he had in his possession and could frequently be seen reading. Willie would repeat it as a poem, on the job or in the bunkhouse, to any of his workmates, or at home to any of his visitors should they requested it.

In light of some vicious rumors that surfaced occasionally which cast aspersions on Willie's military service, Willie's love for the poem may seem a little unusual. Of course, most people who knew Willie also knew that he was a teetotaler, and in his testimonies in the Methodist after-service he often expressed his gratitude to his God for Divine Grace in that regard.

Given the nature of his military service and some of the less than charitable things that were said about him, his father, who crossed Jordan in the mid-fifties, countered by saying that he had never known Willie to take a drink, even before his son had become an enlisted military man, and that. moreover, Will had gotten saved when he was a wee lad.

The Drinking House Over the Way

The room was so cold, so cheerless, and bare
With its rickety table and one broken chair,
With its curtainless window with hardly a pane
To keep out the snow, the wind, and the rain.

A cradle stood empty, pushed up to the wall
And somehow that seemed the saddest of all.
In the old rusty stove, the fire was dead
There was snow on the floor at the foot of the bed.

And there, all alone, a pale woman was lying
You need not look twice to see she was dying
Dying of want, of hunger and cold,
Shall I tell you her story, the story she told:

No, ma'am, I'm no better, my cough is so bad
It's wearing me out though, and that makes me glad,
For 'tis wearisome living when one's all alone.
And Heaven, they tell me, is just like a home.

Yes, ma'am, I've a husband, he's somewhere about,
I hoped he'd come in 'fore the fire went out,
But I guess he has gone where he's likely to stay
I mean to the drinking house over the way.

It was not always so, and I hope you won't think
Too hard of him lady, it's only the drink.
I know he's kind hearted, for, oh. how he cried,
For our poor little baby the morning it died.

You see he took sudden, and grew very bad
And we had no doctor, my poor little lad.
For his father had gone, never meaning to stay
I am sure, to the drinking house over the way.

And when he came back, 'twas far in the night
And I was so tired and sick with fright
Of staying so long with my baby alone
And it cutting my heart with its pitiful moan.

He was cross with the drink, poor fellow, I know
It was that, not his baby, that bothered him so.
But he swore at the child as panting it lay
And went back to the drinking house over the way.

I heard the gate slam, and my heart seemed to freeze
Like ice in my bosom and there on my knees
By the side of the cradle, all shivering I stayed
I wanted my mother, I cried and I prayed.

The clock, it struck two, ere my baby was still
And my thoughts went back to my home on the hill
Where my happy girlhood had spent its short day
Far, far from the drinking house over the way.

The Oral and Folk Story Tradition Of Western Notre Dame Bay,
north east coast of Newfoundland Island

Could I be that girl, the heartbroken wife,
There watching alone while that dear little life
Was going so fast that I had to bend low
To hear if he breathed, 'twas so faint and so low.

Yes, it was easy, his dying, he just grew more white,
And his eyes opened wider to look for the light,
As his father came In, 'twas just break of day,
Came in from the drinking house over the way.

Yes, ma'am, he was sober, at least mostly, I think
He often stayed that way to wear off the drink
And I know that he was sorry for what he had done
For he set a great store by our first little one.

And straight did he come to the cradle bed where,
Our baby lay dead, so pretty and fair.
I wondered that I could have wished him to stay
when there was a drinking house over the way.

He stood quite a while, did not understand
You see, 'til he touched the cold little hand,
Oh' then, came the tears and he shook like a leaf
And he said 'twas the drinking that made all the grief.

The neighbors were kind and the minister came
And he talked of my seeing my baby again
And of the bright angels, I wondered if they,
Could see in that drinking house over the way.

Then I thought when my baby was put in the ground
And the men with their spades were shaping the mound
If somebody could only help me to save
My husband who stood by my side at the grave.

If only it were not so handy to drink
The men that make laws, ma'am, sure didn't think,
Of the hearts they would break, of the souls they would slay
When they licensed that drinking house over the way.

I've been sick ever since and it cannot be long,
Be pitiful, lady, to him when I'm gone
He wants to do right, but you never can think
how weak a man grows   when he's fond of the drink.

And it's tempting him here, and it's tempting him there
Four places I've counted on this very square.
where a man can get whisky by night and by day
Not to mention the drinking house over the way.

There's a verse in the Bible, the minister read
No drunkard shall enter the kingdom, it said,
And he is my husband, and I love him so,
And where I am going, I want him to go.

Our baby and I will both want him there
Don't you think the dear Saviour will answer your prayer.
And please, when I'm gone, ask someone to pray,
For him at the drinking house over the way.

One aspect of William Twilling's personality that puzzled people was his propensity to do things without regard to consequences. Most people assumed that it was because of shellshock or what is now known medically as Post Traumatic Stress Disorder.

Willie would simply do things. He never ever considered the consequences of his actions. It was as if he had no notion of taking responsibility for his behaviour. Fortunately, as far as is known at present, anyway, most of his seemingly thoughtless or rash behaviours or actions didn't have fateful consequences - unusual consequences, maybe, but not fateful or fatal. He thought nothing of tumbling a workmate in the water - regardless of season. He took chances, seeming oblivious of the danger. He was the type of person who would try to walk on water even though he couldn't swim.

People were also amazed and no little shocked that at at the funeral of his first wife, Eleanor, he was passing jokes with the pallbearers. He even joked with the men who were working on his son, Alexander, when they were trying to pump air into his lungs. The boy had drowned after he fell over the stage head. It wasn't that the man didn't experience grief. The man was obviously devastated in both situations. It seemed as if he wasn't able to determine appropriate behaviour to fit the circumstances or was incapable of separating, identifying, or appropriately exhibiting his emotions

Modern clinical psychologists would describe his condition as dysfunctional executive powers. Executive powers, the mental mechanisms that enable us - most of us, anyway - to analyze our planned behaviours and determine whether they are appropriate, seemed to be missing from Willie's psychological constitution. Some people suggested that it was likely because of his war experiences, maybe a result of torture in a prisoner of war camp, or some other war experience equally traumatic. To be truthful, several men who knew Willie as boys when they were growing up at Harbour Divine, suggested, unkindly to be sure, that Willie never had any such abilities to start with when he was a boy or later, and that that lack might have contributed to his dysfunctional behaviour or traumatic war experiences, such as they might have been. Most people, however, dismissed such comments as jealousy. Village folk would comment acidly to each other, "Tis not much trouble ta' know that Willey's backbiters were not waarr veterans!"

Some of his spontaneous behaviours were merely amusing, from an objective perspective, naturally. Once, in the early 80s, upon arriving at Toronto airport when he was on his way to Sudbury to visit one of his sons, he walked up to a very pregnant young woman, laid his hand gently on her protruding belly and sweetly asked, "And, my dear, are you wishing for a boy or a girl?" whereupon the lady screamed, security came rushing, and our Willie was arrested before he got to his baggage.

Luckily for Willie, the two security guards were transplanted Notre Dame Bay boys and a brown man with a turban who had no idea what was being said. The two security guards, quickly apprising Willie's origin, interrogated him using the unique phraseology of their natal home. Willie was lucky, that time. These guys understood Willie or, at least, they said they did.

After much questioning, Willie was released to his anxious son who biting his cheek so that his father couldn't see his mirth, asked, rather sarcastically, "Well, Dad, what the diggins did you do this time?" (Only, he didn't say "diggins"!)

Willie was too shamedface to respond but merely shook his head. Even Willie was sometimes appalled at his own behaviour - in hindsight, of course, and after someone had pointed it out. But, it never seemed to make any difference.

On several occasions, Willie's sons got him out of trouble while accompanying their father in his visits to the big city by explaining to aghast Torontonians - those who never commit faux pas ! - that Willie was their retarded uncle. Willie seemed to think that those antics that elicited laughter at Harbour Divine or in a bunkhouse of all males would be equally appreciated by big city people. He failed to understand that the people of Harbour Divine, unlike those of the big city, had a sense of humour. As it was, when he made some rather loud comments about the different dress codes of some of Toronto's ethnic population, he was lucky to get off without being lynched, celebrated war hero or not.

Willie was an outstanding carpenter. Had he been able to read a bit better, who knows what he might have done in life? As it was, he was not afraid to take on jobs that he might, more wisely, have left to people with more appropriate education and training.

Take the time, for example, in the late 70s when there was a great push on in Grand Falls and Gander and Deer lake and

190

Tales from Harbour Divine
*The Oral and Folk Story Tradition Of Western Notre Dame Bay,
north east coast of Newfoundland Island*

Lewisporte and Corner Brook and Clarenville and Carbonear and Mount Pearl and St. John's, and in twenty or thirty other towns, to construct subdivisions or to install new water and sewer systems. Willie had worked on about a dozen water and sewer projects around the province over a five or six year period prior to this adventure. On this particular occasion Willie was a labourer on a water and sewer project at Town One. (It might be unfair to identify the exact town, or the precise subdivision or the exact date. Innocent people might be embarrassed. It has also been opined that there might even be insurance issues should the exact circumstances become known). Anyway, the project engineer died suddenly of a massive coronary event, as the workers were told. "Dat means 'art attack, byes," one of the workers was quick to explain. He was a Knight from Jackson's Cove.

The town manager, Paul Narlson, called the workers together: "Gentlemen, I'm afraid you are going to have to be let go, all of you. We are not able to get a civil engineer anywhere in the province. Every blessied one of them is too busy. So we have to shut down the project until one becomes available. That might not be until next spring. We are even advertising in the *Globe and Mail*, but our chances of getting one is very slight. It seem that every available civil engineer is gone to northern Alberta where they are building that big oil refinery."

Willie and his buddies needed the work. It was only about another couple of months to completion of that water and sewer project. Without it, they wouldn't have enough stamps for unemployment benefits.

"So what is the problem?"

The town manager turned to look at William Twilling. "We can't finish the job without the civil engineer."

"Sure, my man, daass not a problem. I can finish the project."

"You can? Do you have civil engineering training?"

Now that Willie had committed himself, he continued, rushing headlong, heedless of the implications of the claims that he was probably not even aware that he was about to make. It was as if someone else made the claims and he had to pretend it was him: "well, I'm not fully trained if'n dass wat you means. I don't have alla me peapers, but," looking around at his work mates, "I'm sure we would have no trouble finishing up this project."

The town manager had already received flack from his town council because they were over budget and behind schedule. Narlson just wanted to get the danged project over and done with. People were clamouring that they wanted to get their houses started. "Well, Mr. Twilling, if you think you can complete this project, then the job is yours. I'll get you to sign the papers and give you the appropriate salary." It was, absolutely, the most money that Willie was ever to make at one time for his entire life - to wit: a civil engineer's salary!.

But, money wasn't his major problem; getting the job done was! Although Willie had seen a blueprint before, her had never actually looked at one. When he tried to do so, he could make neither head nor tail of the drawings in the engineer's shack. Moreover, he couldn't read the pile of correspondence and documentation. All those forms!

192

Tales from Harbour Divine
The Oral and Folk Story Tradition Of Western Notre Dame Bay,
north east coast of Newfoundland Island

Willie knew he had a problem. How the juiss did he get into this mess? He realized that it wasn't the first time that his mis-speaking had gotten him into metaphorical raw sewer, but this might be the one most difficult from which to extricate himself.

Willie called the workers together. They all crammed into the engineer's shack as he explained that if they were to keep their jobs and get enough stamps for their UI, then they needed some kind of miracle. He explained his lack of skills and competencies. It was, likely, the most humble moment of his life. One is led to wonder if, just maybe, on that occasion, consequences of behaviours might have crossed his mind.

"Now then, " said Will. "Anybody here can read?"

"I can read well enough. I went to Probationers Summer School and was teaching at Roberts Arm and Hearts Delight for four years."

Willie turned to look at Junior Penting from Harry's Harbour. "Can you write, too?"

"Oh, yes!"

"Good, you'm in charge of all readin' and ritin' and takin' notes and fillin' in alla dose farms. But you still got to work, too. Okey?"

"Fine with me!"

"Now, anyone can read doze bloomin' blueprints and drawins?"

"I did one year of drafting at trade school. I'm goin' back again next September to finish up."

"Well, my son," Willie said to Mansfield Payne from Pilley's Island, "You know wat you'm in charge ov, if'n you'v got the guts ta do ut???"

"I can do it!"

"Good! I knowed yer faader on the Labrador. He's a good man. He'll be proud a' ya."

In likewise manner, Willie determined the special skills of each of his workers, assigned them specialized jobs if they were willing to take them on, and sent them to work.

The town manager was absolutely amazed. He had never seen such an organized work site before, and he had certainly never seen so much work done in such a short time. Not only did the crew get the project back on schedule, but they finished the job two weeks earlier than had been projected. The finished project was a star in Narlson's crown.

On the Wednesday of the last week, Narlson got a call from Jason Bilings, town manager of Town Two. Town Two water and sewer project had stalled because their civil engineer had become ill. Bilings called Narlson to ask the status of the Town One project. Hearing that Town One's project was finishing up at week's end, Bilings jumped in his car and headed for Town One, getting there in grave-yard tempting time. Accompanied by Narlson, Bilings arrived on site just as the men were putting away their tools for the day. Willie and Bilings were introduced.

194

Tales from Harbour Divine
The Oral and Folk Story Tradition Of Western Notre Dame Bay,
north east coast of Newfoundland Island

"Mr. Twilling, I understand that you've done a good job, here. We are looking for a good qualified civil engineer such as yourself to come to Town Two and finish up our water and sewer project. Uh, where did you study engineering?"

Willy had never in his life been stuck for an answer to a question. Many times, he lived to regret having said answers. But, answers he had, immediately.

"Um, in Ontario."

"Ontario? Where? "

Willie hesitated. He knew there was some kind of college or something at Sudbury because he had been there several times to visit his son. "Oh, at Sudbury."

"Sudbury? At the college or university? Did you do the engineering degree or only the diploma?"

Willie was uncomfortable. This man knew too much. Could he claim a degree? He knew that he was digging himself in a hole. The man had said only a diploma. A diploma must be somehow less than a degree. "Oh, bie, just the diploma."

"Oh, the Diploma in Civil Engineering Technology at Cambrian College?"

Willie was sweating. How much could he say. But he was grateful that Bilings was providing the answers for him. "Yes, technology. Yes, Cambrian College." He'd never heard of the place before.

"Good school. That'll do for us."

How the heck was he going to get out of this one? He stalled. What could he say?

"Got a good crew a men, I suppose? "

"Oh, yes! We need only an engineer. We'd have a riot on our hands if we brought in any workers from outside. A lot of the guys got tired of waiting around and have gone of to northern Alberta, to Fort McMurray. Some even quit the job, here, to go up there. A lot more money."

"Thank the Lord God almighty!" Willie said to himself. Bilings had just given him his way out.

"Well, that's really funny. But, sir, I regret that I can't take the job - as much as I'd like to. You see, just last night I got a call from Fort McMurray. I'm leavin' to go to Alberta on Monday. I expect I'll be seeing some of your guys, there."

****

George, William's oldest son, is a welder by trade. George is intelligent and aware. Besides, he reads quite a lot, subscribes to a number of magazines, uses the Internet, and so on.

In the late 80s, George asked his father, then in his 70s, why he didn't go to some of the Canadian Legion functions or go to some of the schools when he was asked. It took some time before Willie could swallow his pride and answer his son's question. It turned out that Willie didn't have any medals. Even though he was now receiving his veteran's stipend and had the veterans' medical card, and so on, Willie was embarrassed. How could he go marching with all of those other guys who had all

196

Tales from Harbour Divine
The Oral and Folk Story Tradition Of Western Notre Dame Bay,
north east coast of Newfoundland Island

of those service medals pinned to their chests? He would be gawked at, made fun of. No, he just couldn't do it.

"Neither medal, father?"

"Nar one!"

"Not one?"

"Not one!"

"Well that is funny. A war veteran with neither medal at all. How come you don't have a medal?"

"I guess I don't deserve one."

"It seems to me," said George, "that every war veteran should have at least one medal. Good God! How come you don't have one?"

It was several days before a reticent William Twilling, war veteran, told his son his military history. George was astounded.

George knew that the villagers at Harbour Divine thought they understood why Willie would not talk about his military service. Some suspected he had been occupied behind German lines - Sabotage! Espionage! Like on TV. Others thought that Willie had been with Military Intelligence and must have worked with the resistance in France. Others though both. Others had heard rather gruesome stories that caused soldiers to become shell-shocked. They imagined that Willie must have seen horrors just too gruesome and traumatic, so much so that it was just much too painful for Willie to try to remember the terrible incidents.

They understood and sympathized with their war veteran. The villagers understood why Willie couldn't talk about it.

Take Lester Tucker, for example, he didn't talk about his military service at all. The only time Lester would talk about his experiences was when he had a few drinks in. They he would talk about being caught between lines and lying low with bullets whizzing over his head. He would weep as he talked about being in the French farmer's field and how the bullets cut down all of the cabbages so that, after about a half hour or so of the barrage, it looked as if someone had made several truckloads of coleslaw and spread over the field.

Lester Tucker also talked about the time he and his bodies were well behind German lines doing reconnaissance and captured a dozen or so German soldiers, very early one morning near the end of the war. The Germans turned out to be a bunch of teenagers, several no more than thirteen or fourteen years old. Tucker's unit was under orders to take no prisoners and not to reveal their presence. What could they do? Lester said that they made the boys strip to their underwear and made them dig their graves. The boys were sobbing and crying as they realized what was going to happen to them. Lester said that most of his company withdrew to new positions, leaving only three men with machine guns to finish the work on the boys. Lester said that he was in command and that the first thing he did was make the boys throw all of their clothes in the hole, then their guns (magazines emptied) and other equipment. Then, said, Lester, "I told them to Lauf! Rennen Sie schnell weg! Ich werde das langsamste schießen! Which means, he said, "Run! Run away

198

Tales from Harbour Divine
The Oral and Folk Story Tradition Of Western Notre Dame Bay,
north east coast of Newfoundland Island

quickly. I'll shoot the slowest one." And, he said, "They ran! I didn't have the heart to shoot at them."

This was the milk that nourished the culture of the village. Not only was Lester Tucker a hero, but he spoke German and disobeyed an unjust order. How fortunate these people were to have such a compassionate man in their midst!

The people of the village also respected Nathan Heath when that ex-military man didn't want to talk about his experiences. Some of the older people still remembered how Nathan and his twin brother, Edgar, went off in 1941 and signed up and went overseas. The two nineteen year old boys were with the same division but were in different companies. One day, in 1943, Nathan was designated one of the machine gunners with his unit shortly before they got into a fight with a German troop. His company ended up killing a number of the enemy before about twenty of the Germans surrendered. They were taking the German prisoners of war back behind Allied lines when they came across a farmhouse. Nailed to the side of the barn were seven Allied soldiers, some of them gutted and partially skinned. One of the bodies was that of Edgar.

The Lieutenant called a halt and directed several of the men to take the bodies down. Others were to dig graves; others to guard the prisoners. Nathan was one of the latter group.

It wasn't nice what happen next, but maybe understandable. Nathan, overcome with anger and grief, opened fire on the prisoners with his machine gun and killed every last one of them. He shot so many bullets into them that the top half of the bodies were falling over before the legs fell down. He went on firing until he ran out of bullets. Then he began to scream and went absolutely berserk. It took four men to hold him down. The Lieutenant said that the incident would have to be reported and demanded that Nathan apologize to the Lieutenant, his superior officer, for not strictly following orders. He had been designated to guard the prisoners, not shoot them!

Nathan apologized.

Nathan later learned that, indeed, the Lieutenant did make a report on Nathan Heath. Several days afterward, a general and several other high ranking officers arrived in their sector. First the Lieutenant, and then Nathan, were summoned to the headquarters tent. Nathan has no idea what the Lieutenant said, but when he went in, saluted, and was told to stand at ease, the general told him that he was receiving the *Medal of Valour.*

The people of the village were proud of Nathan. They were likewise proud of Willie, even if they didn't quite know the nature of the latter soldier's military service. All they could remember was that Willie had, initially, been declared dead and that he had been gone little more than two years when he had returned home severely wounded and had taken several more years to fully recuperated. He was not able to return to the fishing boat until well after the end of the war.

George was gratified – if a little puzzled – to hear his father's story. He determined that his father deserved some medals.

The first medal that George made for his father was in 1990. He made it by welding a clasp to one of the commemorative

200

Tales from Harbour Divine
The Oral and Folk Story Tradition Of Western Notre Dame Bay,
north east coast of Newfoundland Island

medallions that almost everybody received on the day that Queen Elizabeth II was crowned on June 2, 1953. In fact, by that day, a mere six years after the war, Willie was already well-healed of his wounds, had married, had several children, and had undertaken to be games chairperson for the children when Harbour Divine had its celebratory garden party. He played *Farmer in the Dell* with the children; *London Bridge is Falling Down; Button the Button, Who Got the Button; Poor Puss and Tell me a Secret.*

Willie had been the life of the garden party! Nobody could stop themselves from smiling when Willie played the Poor Puss. He could contort his face in so many strange configurations that almost all of the adults standing around outside the children's circle were laughing uproariously as the children gamely tried – and failed - to keep a straight face as the game required.

George found the design for the Newfoundland service colours of the British military, and George's mother created one for Willie with fabric she had on hand and using her sewing machine. Did a good job of it to! George pinned it to his father's chest, told him he was proud of him and kissed him on the cheek. Willie wept with pride, but still couldn't attend any formal functions. But, he loved that medal. He made a little glass fronted case for it and hung it on his bedroom wall.

In 1996, George discovered a French *Croix de Geurre* for sale in one of his Military History magazines. He sent off $65.00 for it to a place in Virginia. When it arrived, he presented it to his father, pinned it to his father's shirt and kissed him on the cheek and told him he was proud of him. Willie was overcome with gratitude. He even put both medals on his shirt and kept them there for the rest of the day.

Coincidentally, the Rev. Joseph Harkness, fresh out of divinity school in Toronto and freshly minted as United Church minister, newly assigned to Harbour Divine Pastoral Charge, came to call that very afternoon because he wanted William, now on the UC Session, to take the Sunday evening service. How could the minister miss the medals that Willie had forgotten to remove? How could he not comment on them?

He immediately asked Willie what the medals represented. Willie was at a loss. What could he say? Alfreda, his wife, jumped into the breach and explained that the first medal was for British service and that it was hanging from *Newfoundland Service Colours*. She also explained that the other medal was the French *Croix de Geurre*. The man of the cloth, suitably impressed, did not ask Willie how he had come by the medals, but made his own assumptions. Willie did not know how to tell the cleric the real story. The reverend gentleman had prayed and taken his leave before Will had determined how to approach the subject. When the minister left, Willie assumed that the issue was over with and put his medals back , both sharing space in the glass-fronted box on the bedroom wall.

The minister, however, coming to his own conclusions, had not forgotten such a significant phenomenon. Willie suspected that something was up when the minister met him at the church door and asked him if he would read the morning's scripture. This Sunday morning it was to be John 15. Willie, of course, obliged, as he was expected to do as a Priest of the Order of

Melchizadech. Neither was Willie surprised when the minister began his sermon and announced his focal text: John 15, 13 - 14: *Greater love hath no man than this, that a man lay down his life for his friends. Ye are my friends, if ye do whatsoever I command you.*

The minister then launched into a wonderful sermon in which he talked about the obvious. Surely he must have been stuck for ideas because then he began a long - although inspiring, of course - explanation of the *Croix de Geurre* and how great an honour it was for the Government of the Republic of France to designate an individual to be accorded such recognition. Then came the moment that Willie, by now, knew was coming - and dreading.

"And, now, dear people, I am absolutely certain that you will be thrilled to learn that one of our very own has been so recognized for his services during the war. The honoured man is no less than our very own William Twilling. Stand up, Mr. Twilling. And be recognized by your congregation."

What could Willie do? He couldn't very well launch into a big explanation of how the minister misunderstood and so on and so on, now, could he?

So, what did Willie do?

He did the only thing that any right-minded military man could do. He stood up to the thunderous ovation of people who had known and admired him for decades.

The community was awed! Teachers at the high school gave students in history and English assignments on various related topics such as: What is valour? What constitutes service to one's fellow man? What is the significance of the *Croix de Geurre?* And so on. At the elementary school, children consulted their encyclopedias and drew pictures of the award, all of which were sent in a package to the humble Willie. He had been asked to come to assemblies at both schools, but he simply couldn't! Everybody understood.

Then, the Ladies Aid had a special dinner with Willie as the guest. He couldn't refuse to go, being a member of the church and all. The legion offered to have another dinner, but Willie pleaded humility. They understood.

Oh, Harbour Divine was thrilled with their newest hero.

But, Willie still couldn't attend public functions in his capacity as war veteran. He felt that it would be disingenuous somehow.

Time moved on .....

In the meantime, the Harbour Divine branch of the Canadian Legion closed its doors. The younger veterans moved away seeking employment; the older veterans were dying off. By 1998, with the death of Clarence Tizzard, William Twilling was the last war veteran of Harbour Divine. Willie went to the funeral and as Mr, Tizzard's coffin was being lowered into the soil Willie was seen to give his old comrade the military salute. Many people became emotional at the sight.

George, the son, now using the Internet, discovered another medal for sale. He sent to England for a German *Iron Cross,* the World War I version that did not have the swastika. That old

204

Tales from Harbour Divine
*The Oral and Folk Story Tradition Of Western Notre Dame Bay,
north east coast of Newfoundland Island*

medal, if one doesn't look too closely, is almost indistinguishable from the American *Cross of Valor* and even the new Canadian *Victoria Cross*. George, now 56 years old, presented his father, once again, with a military medal. His father was overjoyed.

Now, William Twilling was the last veteran of Harbour Divine. It was a matter of a few days when the principal of the high school came to see Willie to request his attendance at a divine service and commemoration of Armistice Day. Willie knew, now, that he could no longer refuse.

George took Willie to *Riff's Ltd* at Grand Falls and the man purchased a new pair of gray slacks, a spiffy blue double-breasted blazer, a new white shirt and a tie with diagonal stripes of red and blue. Will got a new haircut, and George shined up his shoes. As Willie was leaving the house, leaning on his walking stick, followed proudly by his missus, about to get into George's car for the ride to the school, George stopped him. Out of his pocket, George retrieved Willie's medals and pinned them on his father's chest. What a wonderful display they made!

Willie was the man of the hour! The belle of the ball, in a sense. After the ceremony people crowded around Willie and complemented him on his outfit and praised him for his medals. Nobody missed the *Iron Cross*, but nobody knew what it was or its significance. Moreover, nobody had the nerve to ask him. That is, not until little Shelly Newman, Grade X, asked Mr. Twilling for an interview for the school newspaper, *The Harbour Divine Forward Thinker*.

"What's this round medal for, Mr. Twilling?"

"British service, my dear, with the Newfoundland Service Bar."

"I knows what that other one is for. I wrote an essay on it. That's the *Croix de Geurre*. But what is this one?"

The crowd around the twosome held its breath. What was it for?

"That, my dear, is for Germany service."

At last people's suspicions were confirmed. Their own William Twilling had been behind German lines during the war, engaged in intelligence gathering and espionage. They had suspected it all along!

The following week, both *The Norwester and The Lewisporte Pilot,* local weekly newspapers that never miss significant events, each carried a photo of the event, both showing William Twilling surrounded by a veritable mob of admiring villagers.

From that time on, William Twilling never hesitated to take his place on the podium at all sorts of commemorative events. At one occasion, even the premier, Mr. ... well, you know who it was! ... attended and was quietly advised that he was in the presence of greatness. After the dinner, the premier came up to Willie and told the former soldier how delighted he was to greet such a distinguished military gentleman. Few voters, indeed, who saw that exchange, voted for the opposition party at the next election.

The years wore on, as the years are wont to do, and they took their toll on William Twilling just as they had done on his compatriots. Willie had, after a long and interesting life, entered

206

Tales from Harbour Divine
*The Oral and Folk Story Tradition Of Western Notre Dame Bay,
north east coast of Newfoundland Island*

his dotage.   However, even in the last year of his life, even if he sometimes needed two men to help him up over the steps to the platform, Willie continued to attend events and continued to proudly wear his medals.

It is true, now, that Willie did look a little sheepish, at times, when the distinguished speaker called attention to him and singled out his Croix de Geurre. But Willie accepted it with the best grace that he could muster. He had never told a lie about either his military service nor about his medals. People could come to their own conclusions and believe what they liked. It wasn't his responsibility to set them straight and cause confusion. People need their heros. Besides, there is no law that prevents anyone who chooses from wearing whatever regalia one wishes. This is a free country and we are free to express ourselves as we please, provided nobody is harmed. And if we give people pleasure and assist their sometimes flagging loyalty or patriotism, then so much the better.

Willie died three years ago at the age of 86. His funeral was well attended. In both the sermon and the eulogy respectful reference was made to William Twilling's *Croix de Geurre* and other distinguished awards. After the brief internment service, a group of young men, using a variety of weaponry and powder-shells, gave William Twilling an appropriate military salute. A volley of sixteen blasts had to mean something! Just why Willie did not have an appropriate colour party from the Canadian Armed Forces to be pall-bearers for Willie and to fire the appropriate salute, nobody could understand.

****

The big question, now, is: should the story of William Twilling's military career be revealed? His son, George, says that he has no problem with it. He considers his father a hero. In fact, after Willie died, George did some investigation and discovered that William Twilling did, in fact, qualify for a service medal. Nobody at the medals and awards division of the federal Department of Veterans Affairs could explain exactly why the award had languished for decades in a folder in a drawer and why it wasn't delivered to the designated recipient when he was still alive. It is now in George's possession.

William Twilling left Harbour Divine on the *Clyde* in late May, 1941. He had been in collar with his father since early March, intending to go to the Labrador. But, when the *Clyde* entered the harbour, southbound, William Twilling knew that duty called. He kissed his mother, shook hands with his father, and entered on the journey of a lifetime.

Arriving in St. John's after his voyage to Lewisporte on the *Clyde*, his train ride from there to Notre Dame Junction, and then the cross-island train to St. John's, William Twilling caught a taxi to the recruiting office, signed the papers, and was sent off to training to Buckmaster's Field - now crudely disappeared under a housing development.

William was a model soldier and received recognition in the form of a sleeve swatch for his prowess in marksmanship. All those long days out in punt, swatching, had then served an additional service in addition to the mere gathering of swiles.

208

Tales from Harbour Divine
The Oral and Folk Story Tradition Of Western Notre Dame Bay,
north east coast of Newfoundland Island

Willie's company was ready to sail to Britain in October, 1941. *The Royal Horseman,* a converted luxury liner, had arrived from Halifax under escort on Tuesday, October 21, carrying a contingent of five hundred Canadian soldiers. On the morning of Wednesday, October 22, they had all tucked into an ample breakfast – the last breakfast in Newfoundland some of these soldiers would ever have, and the last Newfoundland breakfast for almost five years for most of the remainder. With a cloudy haze rolling up off to the easterd, shortly after nine o'clock, with their kits slung over their backs, Four hundred Newfoundlanders proudly marched up the gangplank of the *Royal Horseman.* They found their assigned places and hammocks, stowed their gear and settled in for the long voyage, cast off scheduled for 8 PM.

William Twilling was excited. One of his training sergeants had told him that his expertise and leadership abilities had been noted and that he could anticipate promotions in short order. Moreover, he had made many friends, and his new buddies, several from his part of Notre Dame Bay, cherished Larry's skills with singing and reciting poetry. In particular, they were amazed at his ability to recite, almost faultlessly, the seventy verse poem, Gondoline, the last one that he had memorized, after copying it out of a book that he had come across while visiting the new *Gosling Library ,* down on Duckworth Street, on one of his weekend passes. One or other of the newly-minted privates would hold the paper and follow along just to make sure that Will didn't cheat.

The men were called to mess for dinner after which they went off to their berths and settled in for an afternoon of innocent fun, telling stories, singing, and so on. Most of the Canadians had been given passes to see the city and were now wandering back aboard ship, some of them weaving slightly and not a few looking rather disheveled. The Newfoundlanders winked at each other and a few of them were making catcalls over the rail to the grinning Canadian soldiers: "I bet Rosie Blue got your pants off before you could get yer money out!" and "That Lucy Minnifen is a man's woman – any man's woman! Looks like she got the better of youse!" and so on, the men naming, individually, the seemingly numerous young ladies who were happy to accommodate the randy young men provided, of course, that the said young men were generous with a share of their stipends. Just how the Newfoundland boys knew about these ladies is a real mystery!

Right after supper, just as their sergeant was about to dismiss them from, one of the officers who were accompanying them overseas came to the enlisted men's mess, demanded their attention and read an announcement. The *Royal Horseman* would not be casting off as scheduled. The convoy they were to join out of Halifax was late. New cast off time was six in the morning of Tuesday, October 23. Thus, any man wanting a pass could get one from their sergeant. They were all to report back aboard ship by twelve midnight for roll call.

Another evening to be entertained by Rosie and Lucy and the other young ladies! How could any red-blooded Newfoundland boy resist. Off they trooped, despite the cold drizzle that was now drifting in from the North Atlantic, some of the lads in search of the girls, others to the nearest drinking establishment. To each his own! Willie knew what he wanted!

210

Tales from Harbour Divine
*The Oral and Folk Story Tradition Of Western Notre Dame Bay,
north east coast of Newfoundland Island*

Sometime after half past eleven, the boys stumbled and sang and hollered themselves back aboard ship, some of them requiring the supporting arm of their comrades. But, even if burping and farting and giggling, they managed to yell out their, "here, sir!" as their name was called or, if they were a bit too much under the weather, one of their supporting buddies would yell out for them. "Abbot! Here sir! ... Anstey! Here, Sir!, Anthony, B! Here Sir! Anthony, K! Here, Burp! Sir! ... Hartery! Here, Sir! .. and so on through the alphabet... Sansome! Here, Sir! ... Tucker! Here, Sir!, Twilling! ..... silence ..... Twilling, W!!. The sergeant thundered. No response. The boys looked around themselves. Where was their Willy?

"Where in tarnation is Willie Twilling?"

The sergeant was angry. "Jameson, Newton, go up to your berths and see if Willie came in early. He may be asleep, If he is, haul his ass down here."

The soldiers looked at each other in consternation. Several of them whispered among themselves that they had seen him shortly after they had gone ashore.

"Silence! If you know of the whereabouts of Twilling, William, tell me! Now!"

Nobody answered. Some shuffled their feet; others shrugged their shoulders back and forth as if to make their uniforms more comfortable. They were all looking at the sergeant as he finished the roll call. Bob Jameson and Charles Newton returned to announce that William Twilling was nowhere to be found.

The men were dismissed. The sergeant consulted with his superior officer. The other company commanders were advised and every berth was searched. The ship was searched. There was no sign of Twilling, William, except his kit which had been carelessly tossed on his hammock just prior to his last trip down to the delights of the city.

Twilling, William was declared AWOL, the base was notified, the Military Police were notified, the city's Constabulary was notified. The *Royal Horseman* cast off at 6 AM and was escorted by the tugboats out of the harbour and into the stream to join the convoy out of Halifax.

On Sunday afternoon, several teenage boys were playing down on the waterfront. They had slipped under the locked wire mesh gate at Steers Cove and were scrounging around, hoping to find something, anything, that might be edible or otherwise salable for a few pennies. Josh Youngston tripped on a broken plank and fell flat on his face. As he was picking himself up, his attention was caught by some clothing on the rocks in the ballast bed. Clothing! Should fetch a few pennies, maybe even a twenty cent piece. He called to his buddies and then clambered down over the side of Steers' finger pier and in between the large tarred logs of the ballast bed. He climbed out again, much quicker than he had gone in. White faced, he could hardly get the words out. "There's a dead soldier in the ballast bed."

It was only a matter of mere minutes when the police responded to the boys' frantic alarm. Several of the Royal Newfoundland Constabulary crawled in between the logs and dragged the body out, not taking too much precaution. You

212

Tales from Harbour Divine
The Oral and Folk Story Tradition Of Western Notre Dame Bay,
north east coast of Newfoundland Island

can't hurt a dead body, after all. The body was tossed up on the pier and a ambulance took it off to the morgue of the General Hospital. The police reported that a man in a military uniform was found dead in the ballast bed of Steers' finger pier. There was no identification except the normal swatches of Newfoundland soldiers. This one had two swatches for marksmanship. Inspector Feltham called up the wardroom of Buckmaster's Field requesting that somebody go down to the General Hospital to identify and, subsequently, take possession of the body.

One of the morgue attendants was called in from his Sunday supper and was directed to prepare the still unidentified body for autopsy scheduled for Monday morning and then to put the body into the cooler. A doctor had examined the body and declared the man dead - as if a doctor was needed to confirm such an obvious fact. One of the policemen was heard to declare, "Well, if the poor bugger wasn't dead when we got him, we've banged him around enough to kill him."

While stripping the clothing from the cold body, the experienced morgue attendant noticed (a) that there was no rigour mortis, (b) that the body was badly damaged, some of the damage seeming to have occurred recently, maybe because of the rough handling from its retrieval, and (c) some wounds were oozing blood. The stiff's eyebrows shot up and it blinked a few times. The attendant got a stetoscope and put to the chest of the cold body. There was a heartbeat!

On Monday, the Daily News carried the terse announcement that an unidentified soldier had been found dead. The official police report declared that a fall due to alcohol consumption was the cause of death.

A training officer from Buckmaster's Field stood by the bedside of the unconscious man and identified him as Twilling, William.

The attending doctor and his colleagues determined that the unfortunate young man had both legs broken, one in two places; multiple skull fractures, broken ribs, a punctured lung, damaged spleen, damaged kidneys, numerous cuts and bruises. Miraculously, the heart seemed undamaged and the intestinal system seemed intact. They also determined than at least several of the more serious traumas were caused by the careless handling the body received after it had been discovered and in the process of delivering it to the hospital. They held out no hope that the soldier would live. Moreover, they could detect no evidence of intoxication.

Surgery was conducted; broken bones were bound and put in plaster casts; cuts were sutured, scrapes and contusions were washed and anointed. Although seemingly continuously comatose, one of the nurses discovered that if she put a spoon of food to the soldier's lips, he would open his mouth and swallow. Occasionally, also, the unconscious man seemed to be mumbling something, as if arguing with himself, something like, " sinking stool ... no! .... mmmm .... mmmmm ....bloated toad ... no! ..... blue light .... mmmmm ...wounds .... caldron ...mmm .... no! ... cauldron ...mmmm ...das right ..." The words seemed to be random. One doctor said that it was the hallucinations of a dying man. He had

214

Tales from Harbour Divine
The Oral and Folk Story Tradition Of Western Notre Dame Bay,
north east coast of Newfoundland Island

seen it many times before. The phrase, "blue light" was a dead giveaway, he said.

And, sure enough, as predicted, on Tuesday morning, without ever having attained consciousness, Twilling, William, Pfc, RNR, was declared dead, this time by two doctors. The body was slung on a gurney and carted off to the morgue with orders to prepare it to ship it off to Harbour Divine because navigation was still open. Otherwise, it would have been simply put in a box, collected by the military, rushed to the General Protestant Cemetery accompanied by some or other minister, dropped in a hole with a prayer, and get back home in time for lunch.

The ward room of the military base was advised and, by way of the Colonial Secretary of The commission of Government of Newfoundland, a telegram was dispatched to:

Joseph Twilling, Harbour Divine, Notre Dame Bay,

father of Twilling, William:

Regret to inform you of the death of Twilling, William, due to unfortunate fall resulting in multiple fatal wounds.

The morgue attendant recognized the body as that of the young man that he had sent upstairs two days previously. He felt a little sad. Here was a fine specimen of Newfoundland manhood, tall, broad-shouldered, muscular. It reminded him of his own son, now fighting somewhere in Europe.

In a moment of compassion – uncharacteristic because for his own well being he had always tried to remain detached – he put his hand on the stiff's forehead. He saw an eye flutter!

He quickly put some blankets around the body and hastened to get the man upstairs on the ward.

Consternation was palpable. On two occasions, now, this man had been declared dead, and the person on the lowest rung of the hierarchy had declared him living. There was some question whether the morgue attendants had any business even examining bodies after they had been declared dead. Cooler heads prevailed. The morgue attendant was not disciplined.

The ward room of the base was informed and another telegram was dispatched to

Harbour Divine:

Re: Twilling, William.

Regret error. Twilling, William is a patient at General Hospital at st. John's. Condition critical.

One of the doctors disputed the police report. He said that he had see the soldier when the wounded man had been first sent to the ward, after the initial fiasco. He had detected, he said, no evidence that the man had been drunk. In fact, given the nature of the wounds, his opinion was that the man had been, effectively, murdered and tossed into the ballast bed. A drunken man would not have been able to maneuver himself down there, particularly with the wounds he had, and there was no way the soldier could have sustained such wounds once in that confined space.

216

Tales from Harbour Divine
The Oral and Folk Story Tradition Of Western Notre Dame Bay,
north east coast of Newfoundland Island

The police disagreed. It was not like the lad was somebody important. He was a nobody, an ignorant *baywop*, not even from town. No further investigation was made.

Twilling, William did not regain full consciousness. At no time did he open his eyes. He was still able to eat a little if a spoon were put to his lips. Occasionally, he still mumbled, still seeming to be arguing with himself. Words such as "laughter," "lonely," "breast" could be identified in his mumbling. Sometimes, he seemed to be repeating a phrase several time, seemingly trying to get it right. He never opened his eyes.

On Friday afternoon, October 31, a nurse called a doctor who confirmed that Twilling, William, had, finally, expired. Might as well send him down to the morgue again. Might as well notify the military and listen to their derisive laughter again. The doctor sat by the bed and looked at the man. No harm would be done if the body were left here for awhile. He had heard of stranger things before. There was so much still unknown to medical science. This Twilling, William was a handsome devil! Too bad he didn't even get his chance to serve his country.

Several hours later as a nurse directed two morge attendants to the bed to retrieve the body, she heard, "No! .... no miserly care, ... but ... mmmm,. Misery and care ... mmm."

Twilling, William seemed not ready to call it quits. She quickly went to his bedside and put her hand on his face. His eyes popped open! "Misery and care," he said. The nurse agreed.

From that point, William Twilling was officially back into the domain of the living. Although most of the first several months were spent in a semi-comotose state, the medical people finally realized that William Twilling was reciting a poem, or trying to remember a poem. One of the nurses told him that he had repeated the poem so often that she now knew part of it. Several of the doctors were amused and were repeating some of the lines to each other. It would be July before William Twilling was, now more or less fully conscious, able to repeat for the astounded hospital staff, the complete seventy verses of *Gondoline.*

William was finally released from hospital in September and was able to hobble up the gangplank, supported by another military man, and take a berth on the *Clyde* and proceed on his journey back home to Harbour Divine. The military had seen to it that the man would arrive home in uniform. As far as they were concerned, he had done no wrong.

Before he left the hospital, one of the doctors asked Willie what had happened. Willie explained that he had been lured up an alley by a girl. He grinned and said that he could never resist a pretty girl. He said that he didn't even get so far as get a feel when he heard a noise. He saw two young men. Then, blacked out. He knew nothing else. It was the same story that he told his son, George. He said that he had not been drinking, that he was too intent on having a good time with the girls.

Willie was able to repeat the poem, *Gondoline,* in its entirety until quite late in life. However, in his last two or three years, he began to forget, being able to recall no more than fifteen or twenty verses. Finally, all that he could remember of it was that he remembered being able to recite it.

Farewell, Twilling, William, Pfc, RNR.

You deserve your medals, all of them. We salute you

The End

Note:

A number of people, having heard the story orally, have expressed curiosity about the poem that William Twilling was reciting while on the troop carrier and at hospital - the seventy verse one. My search paid off. Although I had heard William recite the poem, or part of the poem, on several occasions (but many years ago, now), I am confident that the poem provided in the Appendix is the poem of interest.

Advertisement: Awaiting Paradise

The Novel:

Awaiting Paradise: A Bitter Wind
by R. Lloyd Ryan
Brief summary of the novel:

Carolus Froding, an idealistic Swede, arrives somewhat unexpectedly in a village in Notre Dame Bay, Newfoundland, just before WW I. He discovers romance and, seemingly, a charming rustic Eden.

Although outport village life for him is initially satisfying, he is appalled by the grinding poverty and debilitating lack of resources and education of the inhabitants. While the latter are struggling to negotiate their destitution they are shamelessly exploited by predatory Bible-thumpers.

As the young man wrestles agonizingly with his own evolution, religious extremism transforms the abeyant paradise into a veritable Hell, and his world convulses and threatens to collapse in tatters around him.

Written against a backdrop of a people yearning in anticipation for union with the United States as their ticket away from their wretched existence, the story portrays the people and their culture frankly and authentically.

The book is based on numerous folk stories and folk tales from Notre Dame Bay, Newfoundland. Moreover, the book was written with the assistance of interviews with numerous people who lived out their lives in the outports, the fishing villages, of Notre Dame Bay.

About the author:

Rev. Dr. Ronald Lloyd Ryan grew up in the village of Roberts Arm, a tiny fishing village of less than 300 souls, lost in the wilderness of ocean, mountains and forests, in the area now called Green Bay South, part of the Beothuck Coast on the north east coast of Newfoundland Island, the village where he went to school up to Grade XI. Until he was twelve years old, the community was geographically isolated, the winding gravel road being completed to that outport village during the summer of 1958. Before that time, travel and communication was by the ocean during the summer and by dog-team through the forest during the winter. During early Spring and late Autumn, travel was virtually impossible by any means, and communication only by telegraph: 65 cents for 15 words.

65 cents was a lot of money, more than one could give the clergy in a month or, for some, in a year. Consequently, messages of only the most dire sort were transmitted. Even the death of a family member did not warrant the expenditure of that kind of money. Better to wait until "transportation opened" when one could send a letter for two cents postage, even if one had to get the teacher or the clergy to write the tragic news, and even if the two cents had to be borrowed.

Lloyd attended Memorial University, University of Toledo, University of Southern Mississippi in full time attendance, and attended several other institutions in irregular attendance, including Bethany Seminary. He earned the degrees of Bachelor of Science, Bachelor of Education, Master of Education, Doctor of Arts and Doctor of Philosophy. He was elected a full member of the American Psychological Association in 2001.

Dr. Ryan was a career educator and counsellor and taught children in Newfoundland and Ontario. He was an educational administrator and supervisor at the school and district levels for over twenty-five years.

He is a published author.

Having spent his formative years as well as the bulk of his professional career in Notre Dame Bay he absorbed the culture and collected stories of his people. He says "his people" not only because he is related by one or more ancestral roots to "an ungodly large proportion of them" but because he carries around with him such a large number of their stories. Therefore, they are his people by common culture even if not by blood.

He is hoping that the response to the folk stories will be sufficiently significant such that he will be able to leave to posterity a significant and worthwhile quantity.

222

Tales from Harbour Divine
The Oral and Folk Story Tradition Of Western Notre Dame Bay,
north east coast of Newfoundland Island

Appendix

Gondoline
by
Henry Kirk White

The night it was still, and the moon it shone
Serenely on the sea,
And the waves at the foot of the rifted rock
They murmur'd pleasantly,

When Gondoline roam'd along the shore,
  A maiden full fair to the sight;
Though love had made bleak the rose on her cheek,
  And turn'd it to deadly white.

Her thoughts they were drear, and the silent tear
  It fill'd her faint blue eye,
As oft she heard, in fancy's ear,
  Her Bertrand's dying sigh.

Her Bertrand was the bravest youth
  Of all our good king's men,
And he was gone to the Holy Land
  To fight the Saracen.

And many a month had pass'd away,
  And many a rolling year,
But nothing the maid from Palestine
  Could of her lover hear.

Full oft she vainly tried to pierce
  The ocean's misty face;
Full oft she thought her lover's bark
  She on the wave could trace.

And every night she placed a light
  In the high rock's lonely tower,
To guide her lover to the land,
  Should the murky tempest lower.

Tales from Harbour Divine
*The Oral and Folk Story Tradition Of Western Notre Dame Bay,
north east coast of Newfoundland Island*

223

But now despair had seized her breast,
 And sunken in her eye;
"Oh tell me but if Bertrand live,
 And I in peace will die."

She wander'd o'er the lonely shore,
 The curlew scream'd above,
She heard the scream with a sickening heart,
 Much boding on her love.

Yet still she kept her lonely way,
 And this was all her cry.
"Oh! tell me but if Bertrand live,
 And I in peace shall die."

And now she came to a horrible rift
 All in the rock's hard side,
A bleak and blasted oak o'erspread
 The cavern yawning wide.

And pendant from its dismal top
 The deadly nightshade hung;
The hemlock and the aconite
 Across the mouth was flung.

And all within was dark and drear,
 And all without was calm;
Yet Gondoline enter'd, her soul upheld
 By some deep-working charm.

And as she enter'd the cavern wide,
 The moonbeam gleamed pale,
And she saw a snake on the craggy rock,
 It clung by its slimy tail.

Her foot it slipp'd, and she stood aghast,
 She trod on a bloated toad;
Yet, still upheld by the secret charm,
 She kept upon her road.

And now upon her frozen ear
  Mysterious sounds arose;
So, on the mountain's piny top
  The blustering north wind blows.

Then furious peals of laughter loud
  Were heard with thundering sound,
Till they died away in soft decay,
  Low whispering o'er the ground.

Yet still the maiden onward went,
  The charm yet onward led,
Though each big Willing ball of sight
  Seem'd bursting from her head.

But now a pale blue light she saw,
  It from a distance came;
She follow'd, till upon her sight
  Burst full a flood of flame.

She stood appall'd; yet still the charm
  Upheld her sinking soul;
Yet each bent knee the other smote,
  And each wild eye did roll.

And such a sight as she saw there
  No mortal saw before,
And such a sight as she saw there
  No mortal shall see more.

A burning cauldron stood in the midst,
  The flame was fierce and high,
And all the cave so wide and long
  Was plainly seen thereby.

And round about the cauldron stout
  Twelve withered witches stood;
Their waists were bound with living snakes,
  And their hair was stiff with blood.

Their hands were gory too; and red
  And fiercely flamed their eyes:
And they were muttering indistinct
  Their hellish mysteries.

And suddenly they join'd their hands,
  And utter'd a joyous cry,
And round about the cauldron stout
  They danced right merrily.

And now they stopp'd; and each prepared
  To tell what she had done,
Since last the lady of the night
  Her waning course had run.

Behind a rock stood Gondoline,
  Thick weeds her face did veil,
And she lean'd fearful forwarder,
  To hear the dreadful tale.

The first arose: She said she'd seen
  Rare sport since the blind cat mew'd,
She'd been to sea in a leaky sieve,
  And a jovial storm had brew'd.

She'd called around the winged winds,
  And raised a devilish rout;
And she laugh'd so loud, the peals were heard
  Full fifteen leagues about.

She said there was a little bark
  Upon the roaring wave,
And there was a woman there who'd been
  To see her husband's grave.

And she had got a child in her arms,
  It was her only child,
And oft its little infant pranks
  Her heavy heart beguiled.

And there was too in that same bark
  A father and his son:
The lad was sickly, and the sire
  Was old and woe-begone.

And when the tempest waxed strong,
  And the bark could no more it 'bide,
She said it was jovial fun to hear
  How the poor devils cried.

The mother clasp'd her orphan child
  Unto her breast and wept;
And sweetly folded in her arms
  The careless baby slept.

And she told how, in the shape of the wind,
  As manfully it roar'd,
She twisted her hand in the infant's hair,
  And threw it overboard.

And to have seen the mother's pangs,
  'Twas a glorious sight to see;
The crew could scarcely hold her down
  From jumping in the sea.

The hag held a lock of her hair in her hand,
  And it was soft and fair:
It must have been a lovely child,
  To have had such lovely hair.

And she said the father in his arms
  He held his sickly son,
And his dying throes they fast arose,
  His pains were nearly done.

And she throttled the youth with her sinewy hands,
  And his face grew deadly blue;
And the father he tore his thin gray hair,
  And kiss'd the livid hue.

*The Oral and Folk Story Tradition Of Western Notre Dame Bay,
north east coast of Newfoundland Island*

And then she told how she bored a hole
  In the bark, and it fill'd away:
And 'twas rare to hear how some did swear,
  And some did vow and pray.

The man and woman they soon were dead,
  The sailors their strength did urge;
But the billows that beat were their winding-sheet,
  And the winds sung their funeral dirge.

She threw the infant's hair in the fire,
  The red flame flamed high,
And round about the cauldron stout
  They danced right merrily.

The second begun: She said she had done
  The task that Queen Hecate had set her,
And that the devil, the father of evil,
  Had never accomplished a better.

She said, there was an aged woman,
  And she had a daughter fair,
Whose evil habits fill'd her heart
  With misery and care.

The daughter had a paramour,
  A wicked man was he,
And oft the woman him against
  Did murmur grievously.

And the hag had work'd the daughter up
  To murder her old mother,
That then she might seize on all her goods,
  And wanton with her lover.

And one night as the old woman
  Was sick and ill in bed.
And pondering solely on the life
  Her wicked daughter led,

228

Tales from Harbour Divine
*The Oral and Folk Story Tradition Of Western Notre Dame Bay,
north east coast of Newfoundland Island*

She heard her footstep on the floor,
  And she raised her pallid head,
And she saw her daughter, with a knife,
  Approaching to her bed.

And said, My child, I'm very ill,
  I have not long to live,
Now kiss my cheek, that ere I die
  Thy sins I may forgive.

And the murderess bent to kiss her cheek,
  And she lifted the sharp bright knife,
And the mother saw her fell intent,
  And hard she begg'd for life.

But prayers would nothing her avail,
  And she scream'd aloud with fear,
But the house was lone, and the piercing screams
  Could reach no human ear

And though that she was sick, and old,
  She struggled hard, and fought;
The murderess cut three fingers through
  Ere she could reach her throat.

And the hag she held her fingers up,
  The skin was mangled sore,
And they all agreed a nobler deed
  Was never done before.

And she threw the fingers in the fire,
  The red flame flamed high,
And round about the cauldron stout
  They danced right merrily.

The third arose: She said she'd been
  To holy Palestine;
And seen more blood in one short day
  Than they had all seen in nine.

The Oral and Folk Story Tradition Of Western Notre Dame Bay,
north east coast of Newfoundland Island

Now Gondoline, with fearful steps,
  Drew nearer to the flame,
For much she dreaded now to hear
  Her hapless lover's name.

The hag related then the sports
  Of that eventful day,
When on the well contested field
  Full fifteen thousand lay.

She said that she in human gore
  Above the knees did wade,
And that no tongue could truly tell
  The tricks she there had play'd.

There was a gallant featured youth,
  Who like a hero fought;
He kiss'd a bracelet on his wrist,
  And every danger sought.

And in a vassal's garb disguised,
  Unto the knight she sues,
And tells him she from Britain comes,
  And brings unwelcome news.

That three days ere she had embark'd
  His love had given her hand
Unto a wealthy Thane:—and thought
  Him dead in Holy Land.

And to have seen how he did writhe
  When this her tale she told,
It would have made a wizard's blood
  Within his heart run cold.

Then fierce he spurr'd his warrior steed,
  And sought the battle's bed;
And soon all mangled o'er with wounds
  He on the cold turf bled.

230

Tales from Harbour Divine
The Oral and Folk Story Tradition Of Western Notre Dame Bay,
north east coast of Newfoundland Island

And from his smoking corse she tore
  His head, half clove in two.
She ceased, and from beneath her garb
  The bloody trophy drew.

The eyes were starting from their socks,
  The mouth it ghastly grinn'd,
And there was a gash across the brow,
  The scalp was nearly skinn'd.

Twas Bertrand's head! With a terrible scream
 The maiden gave a spring
And from her fearful hiding-place
  She fell into the ring.

The lights they fled—the cauldron sunk,
  Deep thunders shook the dome,
And hollow peals of laughter came
  Resounding through the gloom.

Source: H. K. White's Poetical Works. Boston: Phillips, Sampson & Company, 1850.

Printed in Great Britain
by Amazon

32150724R00131